# SPECIAL PROBLEMS
# IN
# LAW ENFORCEMENT

# SPECIAL PROBLEMS
# IN
# LAW ENFORCEMENT

*By*

**DONALD O. SCHULTZ, B.S., M.P.A.**

*Police Science Instructor*
*Broward Community College, Fort Lauderdale, Florida*

CHARLES C THOMAS • PUBLISHER

*Springfield • Illinois • U.S.A.*

*Published and Distributed Throughout the World by*

CHARLES C THOMAS • PUBLISHER

Bannerstone House

301-327 East Lawrence Avenue, Springfield, Illinois, U.S.A.

Natchez Plantation House

735 North Atlantic Boulevard, Fort Lauderdale, Florida, U.S.A.

*With THOMAS BOOKS careful attention is given to all details of
manufacturing and design. It is the Publisher's desire to present books that are
satisfactory as to their physical qualities and artistic possibilities and
appropriate for their particular use. THOMAS BOOKS will be true to those
laws of quality that assure a good name and good will.*

*Printed in the United States of America*

*RN-1*

*Dedicated
to Those Police Officers
Whose First Loyalties Are
to Principles,
not Men*

# PREFACE

THE enforcement of the law has never been nor will ever be an easy task. The police community has, however, evolved further in the last few years than the total of its achievements prior to our enlightened era.

Many tools and scientific advances are now in use which have elevated the level of proficiency in criminal investigation and other areas of police work to an outstanding degree. Data processing is but an example of what is available to the modern-day police agency. With all the advances that have occurred in law enforcement, it is hard to realize that we are but at the threshold of our possibilities.

Even though advanced technology had been adapted to the needs of the modern-day police agencies for every advance which makes the job of law enforcement scientifically easier, two barriers have been placed to plague the police. The rapid pace of change has been a double-edge sword. Scientific assistance has been outweighed by problems which were nonexistent a short time ago, but now are stalking the very steps of each policeman throughout our nation.

The purpose of this text is to delve into the various problems which the law enforcement community must cope with today. Some of these areas of concern are recent in the history of law enforcement. Others are recurring situations which must be explored and understood. In many cases there are no black and white guidelines to go by, and by their very nature, many specialized problems offer none for future reference. Of major importance, however, is that each police officer and administrator be able to recognize the basic problems and be able to intelligently decide on what course he and his agency should take. This text, then, is not directed toward the basic problems, but toward the uncommon situations which are not part of the daily routine of law enforcement.

Realizing that many specialized problems in law enforcement will be governed by geography, racial distribution, economics, and on some occasions by a degree of political influence that can be exerted upon the operational elements of police activities, it is necessary to approach many of the specialized problems with a general approach rather than a direct problem-solution format.

# CONTENTS

# SPECIAL PROBLEMS
# IN
# LAW ENFORCEMENT

# Chapter 1

# THE POLICE IMAGE
## THE POLICE IMAGE IN GENERAL

THE most important thing to establish in the minds of people today is the positive image of law enforcement. This image is directly reflected in the police officer as an individual protecting the rights, lives, and property of our citizens. More and more today the young people of our nation need an appreciation and understanding of the vital role which the law enforcement officer plays in their daily lives.

## ATTACKS ON THE POLICE

One of the greatest tragedies of our national life today has been the constant undermining of public confidence in the officer of the law. Time after time in mass news media, in political and semipolitical speeches, and even in casual conversations on the street, derogatory and hostile comments toward the police are heard. In more recent years, certain individuals and groups have purposely gone out of their way to hurl scorn and vituperation against police.

Throughout the history of the Communist Party there have been attacks on the law enforcement in this country. The Communist Party and their dupes have falsely charged police as being brutal, and through agitation and propaganda techniques, have attempted to portray all police officers as the enemy of the people. The Party searches for agitational points, attempting to gain support against the police from the non-Communist majority. Their biggest assist comes from those of the so-called liberal element who are always ready to prove their objectivity. To take our nation they must first break down the effectiveness of law enforcement. The officer of the law stands as a barrier to the Communist Party because the police are sworn to protect our free society from the criminal minority and those who would overthrow our system of law.

A number of left wing extremist groups are freely working within our country diligently trying to discredit law enforcement. These "New Leftist" groups are succeeding to a point in giving law enforcement a negative, unattractive public image. They would like nothing more than to sow in the minds of citizens the idea that law enforcement is bigoted, unfair, and corrupt. They have been relentless in their assaults against the police. In recent demonstrations, common words such as "pigs" and "swine" seem to be fair play against the police officer. These names are often reinforced by the most coarse and vulgar obscenities and actions.

During such demonstrations, New Leftists have not hesitated to utilize any weapon possible to attack the officer. The tragedy in these radical concepts and ideas is that even though it represents a small group of extreme misguided militants, it encourages deliberate and provocative violations of the law. To this group the law is something to be obeyed only if it fits their purposes. If for some reason the law does not suit them, they just disobey it. They not only disobey the rules of our society, but at the same time do everything possible to discredit the very role of law enforcement itself. This attitude has become more accepted and is doing an extreme amount of damage to our constitutional structure of government. Frank W. Wilson in this text, *The Law and the Urban Age,* states "if we implant into the minds of citizens, especially young people, the concept that law enforcement is an enemy, that laws are to be obeyed or disobeyed at the convenience of the individual and that civil disobedience is the best way to effect changes in our society, we are sowing the seeds of anarchy and chaos."

Unfortunately, we live in an age of violence. From the years 1960 to 1967, crimes of violence jumped 73 percent. This is indeed a serious reflection of our national life. During the same period of time arrests of juveniles for violent crimes doubled. Crimes are increasing throughout our nation in all areas — urban, suburban, and even in the rural areas.

More and more violence is being used against the law enforcement officer. In 1967, there were seventy-six police officers killed by criminal actions. This high number of police killings was substantially above the annual average of forty-eight established from 1960 to 1966. The addition of seventy-six police officers killed in 1967 raises the toll of these tragic deaths to four hundred and eleven for the period 1960-1967. In addition to deaths, a large amount of duty time is lost from the result of injured officers. These injuries arise not only from criminal action but also from the violence engendered by riots, demonstrations, and other types of disturbances. Never before has the law enforcement community faced such a deliberate and organized violence towards its members.

Unfortunate as it may seem, some groups and individuals feel that change in society can be accomplished only through violence. Professor Bristow in *Effective Manpower Utilization* relates, "Force is becoming a popular student tactic because students are learning that it works." Many believe legal protest is no longer tactically effective. Such a concept that violence is the magic key of effecting change is a deadly germ which is becoming highly infectious. Therefore, if an individual or group does not achieve its aims through legal redress, then simply use force. Some of the more practiced forms of force are the kidnap of a college dean, occupying a school building, invading the college president's office, or if the mood strikes, starting a fire.

There are many organizations such as the Revolutionary Action Movement, the Black Panther Party, as well as the Communist Party, which believe in violence. They seek to instill fear. They appeal mainly to intolerance and irrationality. Inflammatory statements to polarize our country about white power and black power emphasize the dangers of violence in our midst. Student leftists, especially those associated with the Militant Students for a Democratic Society, think in terms of revolution and destruction of our society through a violent overthrow of our system of government.

The strength of our American institutions has always rested on respect for the law and the officers of the law. Change in the system can and has in the past been effected through the orderly processes of government. For any group or individual to take the law into his own hands is to weaken the validity of our system of government. Violence, of course, is part of our daily lives.

Responsible citizens cannot overlook the presence of violence. To do so now would be foolish and self-defeating.

Over the years there have been some tendencies to create heroes out of the criminal element. The hoodlum who carries a gun, who speaks obscene language, is often extolled with high esteem. The criminal is not a glamorous person. He is selfish, interested only in himself, and completely callous of the rights of others. His actions are injurious to family life and demean the concepts of love, justice, and fair play. Crime is a dirty, unscrupulous business which reveals man at his lowest level. To glamorize any person of this nature is a serious miscarriage of moral values.

## THE EFFECTS OF THE MASS MEDIA
## ON LAW ENFORCEMENT

America's mass media are today playing a key role in our free society. They sometimes perform great services. Day after day, through their stories, articles, and programs which are portraying crime in its true light, as a wretched condition which brings misery, despair, and eventually death, they assist the law enforcement struggle. In this way they are responsibly doing their duty. Any mass media presentation which shows a series of unpunished crimes or leaves impressions that crime really does pay can do a grave damage.

These organs of public opinion, with the help of concerned citizens over the nation, can do much to emphasize the wholesome values of our society and to regain the respect for law and the law enforcement officer. This can and will restore the law enforcement officer as the symbol of our republican way of life. The new media must assist law enforcement by giving a true picture of the majority of police officers. The public must be made aware of the fact that police personnel are becoming better trained and more efficient, despite the efforts of the Liberal politicans and Supreme Court decisions to hamper police operations.

## MOLDING AN EFFECTIVE POSITIVE POLICE IMAGE

### Personnel Selection

No police agency can hope to have a good public image unless the basic requirements and selection methods for its personnel are established to insure the hiring of only high-caliber applicants. There is a definite relationship between police personnel selection and the continuing or future image of the agency. Each recruit selected will not only represent his own image, but the image of the entire police department. This point cannot be over-emphasized, as it represents the basic foundation of how the law enforcement image has been created and is maintained.

Police personnel selection lacks uniformity throughout our country; however, the following are basic requirements which must be included for the consideration for each applicant:

1. A basic intelligence level that exceeds that of the average man. With changes ever-present, police personnel must be able to meet new challenges and situations. The above-average-intelligence applicant will be better prepared to intellectually adapt himself.

2. A physical profile including height and weight of reasonable distribution is of importance in communication between the officer and the citizens. Extremely underweight or overweight individuals just cannot command respect as their appearance in a uniform will make a mockery out of what should represent a semimilitary appearance and demeanor. Naturally, an excellent health record is also required.

3. A background investigation on each potential applicant must be a part of the hiring process. No police agency should ever hire a police officer without first completing a comprehensive background investigation on him. A background investigation should include the following:

    a. Confirmation of birth date and place of birth.
    b. Education.
    c. Military service.
    d. Organizational affiliations.
    e. Interviews of listed references and resulting leads.
    f. Employment checks.
    g. Neighborhood evaluation.
    h. A national agency check including all police agencies.
    i. Credit ratings.
    j. Family and marital status.
    k. Any other pertinent information which will reflect the applicants integrity and discretion.

4. An oral interview with the applicant is an effective tool in the selection process. The principal asset of the oral interview is that if handled properly, the candidate's articulation, emotional responses, and any personality oddities can be observed and evaluated. The applicant's ability to use good common sense can also be evaluated through a series of situational questions. Raw intelligence alone is not sufficient in law enforcement. The ability to use good common sense is many times unfortunately overlooked in light of an impressive I.Q. rating.

5. Psychological screening by a psychiatrist trained and experienced in police candidate selection is an expensive but necessary part of the hiring process of an agency concerned with only allowing the best to serve. Deep-rooted mental problems which only a trained psychiatrist can detect are best found during the pre-hiring stage.

6. The probationary period is the final testing ground for the police candidate. Those agencies utilizing the civil service system can properly state that the most effective tool in the personnel selection process is the probationary period. In many agencies the probationary period includes academy stress training which is designed to eliminate the emotionally immature. The emphasis on stress training requires no elaboration, for in most cases where the police image suffered at the hands of a few policemen, it could usually be traced to undeveloped leads that were apparent during the academy period.

A portion of the probationary period will be an evaluation of the new officer's ability on the street. When all is said and done, the best selector and educator is the "street." It is here that a man proves himself to be a good "street policeman," an adequate performer, or unable to do the job. The street is where education and academy-trained police techniques are utilized in real life situations.

## POLICE TRAINING

Police training covers a wide range of areas. Many colleges throughout our nation offer credited courses leading to degrees in police science, law enforcement, or public safety. The majority of these programs are administered and instructed by older professional street policemen who can relate many years of experience into weeks of study. Actual experience may be the best teacher; however, the contribution of the college police science programs cannot be overlooked. Of great importance in the police image creation is the number of police personnel attending college and university programs.

## In-service Training

In-service training sessions within the various police agencies are of great value. Each department can relate to its own personnel the problems and actions to be taken and why. Local situations and specialized problems are discussed so that each member of the agency can have an awareness of what is important in his community. In-service training should minimally include partial techniques and methods, interview and interrogation, crime scene and criminal investigation, law, evidence, juvenile procedures, vice control, and public relations.

## Police Institutes

Two and three full-day study sessions for a large number of policemen from agencies within an acceptable driving distance has proven to be effective as a learning device. Usually specialized law enforcement problems are studied, i.e. vice, arrest, search and seizure, the drinking driver, narcotics, etc. Lately many police institutions have dealt with community relations and the police image.

## Sensitivity Training

Because of a vocal clamor from the Liberal elements during the last few years for "nicer" law enforcement officers, some police administrators decided to give their personnel what is popularly called "sensitivity training." Image-wise it would appear to be some sort of universal answer for law enforcement. Through magazine articles, newspapers, and the rest of the news media, sensitivity training is related to training given so that the police officer is conditioned not to "overreact," but instead show empathy towards the criminal element and to the members of minorities, criminal or otherwise. Even though a good public image is essential to the law enforcement community, we cannot afford to send rookie police officers out into the streets wondering how an armed robber feels, or if he has a family. The police officers must be made more aware of current threats from the militant minority element rather than learning how it feels to be a member of a minority. Too many recent deaths among the newer or rookie police officers indicate that perhaps there may be more emphasis given to sensitivity training and not enough to protection techniques. The death of a police officer has never assisted in the creation of a good police image, and even if it did, the price would be too high. The unfortunate attitude of some of our police administrators can best be exemplified by a quotation from the editorial comment of the *Wisconsin Police Chief,* December 1969–January 1970 issue which in part states, "This is a period of ideas. Time to try something new — *even if it doesn't make much sense."* The editorial comments that besides everything else, sensitivity training is absurd. Thoughtful police administrators can only fully agree with this premise. Police officers already have a type of sensitivity training. They are sensitive to the value of laws and their duties to the victims of crimes to do their best to see that the guilty are apprehended.

The total scope of sensitivity training may best be explored by some comments of the Honorable John R. Rarick of Louisiana when he entered the following for *Congressional Record* on March 11, 1969:

> Mr. Speaker, Lavrentia Beria, the Bolshevik psychopolitician, head of the Soviet secret police under Stalin, talked of a master plan to conquer the world:
>
> "Give us one generation and you'll never be able to catch up."
>
> It becomes more obvious that his plan is now underway in the United States to destroy one generation by removing from our youth the desire to be an individual resulting in loss of the will to resist — lawlessness, immorality; the warping of society, and consequently cultural destruction.
>
> By now most people should understand that the term "human

relations" is a "sliding-off" of identity to camouflage sensitivity training once called brainwashing.

Unless the parents of America become aroused and organize — "sensitivity training" or "group therapy" can well be the weapon to deliver the young generation.

Sensitivity training is a form of group criticism which is being introduced in high schools, colleges and universities, churches, police departments, YMCA groups, summer camps, etc. Described by its advocates as "group therapy," it has aroused widespread opposition wherever it has been used because it employs almost the same method that was used to brainwash American prisoners of war in Korea — organized "group criticism."

Group criticism compels the participant to bare his soul before ten or fifteen other persons who are required to do likewise under the direction of a group leader. The individual is pressed to seek out real or fancied shortcomings in his personality and thinking, to humble himself and give up his independence of mind and judgment, to make himself dependent upon the good opinion of the leader and others in the group.

The individual's "problems" become group property and, as the talk progresses and the group tries to work out solutions, any or all of the following results may take place:

1. After hearing ten to twenty others confess their "faults," one is inclined to feel that his own are not so bad, thus encouraging him to accept lower moral standards.

2. Discovery that one's own or family standards are different from those of the group creates doubts as to whose standards are correct.

3. Individual responsibility and decision-making are discouraged, in fact, penalized, causing one to feel inadequate and unable to make decisions without approval of the group or group leader.

4. Participants are encouraged to bring problems to the group instead of to family and church.

5. One's family is made to seem pretty "square" compared to the consensus of the group.

All such programs are "geared to change"; thus, unless one is of unusual integrity and character, they tend to realign loyalties away from home, family and the church, and cause the individual to conform more nearly to the standards and ideals of the group. This is perhaps an oversimplification, but it is difficult to dispute the fact that group criticism or sensitivity training is a form of brainwashing.

Some years ago, Edward Hunter, author and foreign correspondent who originally introduced the term "brainwashing" into the English language, pointed out:

> The United States is being conditioned to accept military defeat . . . the objective now is to bring about, by a sophisticated Pavlovian approach, consent by the American people and Government for what we have always refused to discuss — battlefield defeat . . . A long, highly skilled campaign has been going on to soften up our people for it. The immediate objective in this war is American acceptance of defeat at the hands of the Vietnam communists. But Vietnam is only one sector of a worldwide front. The long range objective for which defeat in Vietnam is supposed to soften us up, is our acceptance of defeat by the Soviet Union.

Is sensitivity training part of this program? And is there anyone who can say that it is calculated to strengthen the moral fiber of this nation?

# Chapter 2

# POLICE PROFESSIONALISM
## GENERAL OBSERVATIONS

 $T$ HE evolution of law enforcement from an occupation to that of a professional status has been discussed and explored by experts from within the police community as well as by non-police individuals. No clear-cut indication has yet been discovered, perhaps because there is no all or nothing solution to the concept of police professionalism. On one extreme there are those who point with pride to the many accomplishments and advancements of law enforcement within recent years stating that the future is but a bright horizon. The other extreme is represented by those who feel that the nature of police work itself just does not lend itself to the ideals of true professionalism. The answer probably lies somewhere between these two points of view.

## PARTIAL PROFESSIONALISM

There is an area of possibility that the total scope of law enforcement will never become a true profession as most people view the concept of professionalism. There are some aspects or duties which just do not lend themselves to a professional image, and it appears unlikely that the law enforcement community will be able to transfer the responsibilities for the performance of these tasks. The need to engage in physical combat, which occasionally must be done, the handling of drunks, and the myriad of semi- and unrelated errands ranging from escorting the city treasurer to the bank, to the removal of dead animals from the roadway all tend to be negative factors towards police professionalism. The duties of the uniformed street policeman are still in many ways just as they were generations ago except for the addition of many minor jobs which could not be given to another city agency for one reason or another.

Some police functions or divisions do lend themselves to

possible acceptance as a profession in the future. Among these are the following:
1. The administrative staff.
2. The intelligence unit.
3. The public or community relations divisions.
4. The detective division.
5. Police lab technicians.

In these functions future police professionalism is possible if the criteria of the concept of a profession are met. There are certain areas which appear common as basic requirements in those fields which have held the status of a profession.

## SOME BASIC REQUIREMENTS OF A PROFESSION

### Professional Bonds

In professions one can note that there appears to be a professional bond between all or most of its ranks. The medical and legal professions are excellent examples of individual responsibility towards each other. The American Medical Association and the American Bar Association are official voices which maintain order and protection to their own membership.

Historically, police officers have had a strong feeling of brotherhood among all those who effectively serve the law. There has always been a protective force uniting the majority of the street policemen. Racial and religious differences are of small concern, as once a man becomes a police officer he has joined the ranks of probably the most abused minority — the occupational minority of those who maintain law and order.

The great majority of the members of the law enforcement community are politically conservative. Within the last few years a small minority of self-declared Liberals have attempted to infiltrate the brotherhood of street policemen. In the area of professional bonds the police service, however, still stands united, as those who cannot or refuse to think like policemen find a lonely existence in an occupation not meant for them.

### Education

A four- or five-year education is a must for one to enter an area as a professional. A formal college education with degree recognition will bring support of the majority of our society who hold an education as the first criterion of those who command respect. Fortunately, many police science programs have been established throughout our nation. The future growth of these existing programs and the establishment of others are obvious.

### Test of Proficiency

After a formal college education is received, the professions demand final tests to demonstrate the overall knowledge of the student in his field. State bar and medical examinations insure that the college has properly taught the student what he must know to operate as a professional. State certification given to successful candidates is an important part of the creation of the professional image.

### Internship

An attorney may first enter the field of law as a research clerk. The future doctor must spend a portion of his time as an intern to demonstrate his skills. In law enforcement an internship period could be established for those educated police officers who are about to enter one of the professionally orientated functions or divisions. It would basically be an accelerated probationary period for professional law enforcement officers.

### Lateral Entry

Without too many exceptions a police officer who leaves the service of one agency to work for another must begin at the lowest level and lose everything he has earned from time in grade to his retirement plan. The ability for lateral entry of qualified personnel at all levels is an important consideration if law enforcement is to reach any degree of professionalism at all. Of course, basic minimum uniform requirements will also have to be established for each level of law enforcement before lateral entry can be established to any degree.

## An Enforceable Code of Ethics

The accepted code of ethics for law enforcement delves into the basic ethics that all police officers should adhere to. If a police officer or police administrator feels that he is above the law or violates the code of ethics he is usually allowed to resign his position in order not to embarrass the rest of the agency. The expulsion of a dishonest or incompetent police officer through his own letter of resignation is no guarantee that he will not merely apply and possibly be accepted on another police department.

A code of ethics, no matter how admirable in its terminology, is useless unless there is a method of enforcement. This enforcement must come from the profession itself with the ability to censure the offenders.

## SUMMARY

With the aforementioned criteria it is obvious that law enforcement must make many more strides and achievements before at least some of its personnel can truly be accepted as professional. The eventual answer to the question of police professionalism will be a matter which will only be settled in the future. Professionalism can only be achieved through a unified concentrated effort by a majority of the honest and dedicated police personnel throughout our republic.

# Chapter 3

# POLICE ETHICS

Ethical practices are of major concern in the field of law enforcement. The police service is more closely scrutinized and open to more derogatory comments than any other occupational group. There are never any shades of gray concerning a police officer's or a police administrator's ethical practices. Either a police officer or administrator is honest or he is not.

It has been an unfortunate fact that the majority of police officers who are forced to leave law enforcement can trace their difficulties back to credit, liquor, or women. Credit is an easy commodity for police personnel because of the security of their position. Needless to say, a careful eye must be kept on the purchasing power of a usually only adequate salary. Any occupation which involves a great deal of mental strain easily leads to alcohol as an escape mechanism. For an occasional release it may be an acceptable means of therapy; however, dependence on alcohol is not only medically harmful, but occupationally fatal. Women are probably one of law enforcement's biggest problems. Many authors point out the fact that police officers are involved in divorces more than any other occupational group. The basic implications are that policemen just like to "play around." When all the factors regarding the amount of opportunity for extra-marital relationships are weighed, the law enforcement community can be proud of the fact that only a small minority of its members have difficulty in maintaining restraint.

There are some questionable practices that have been used in the police service from time to time. The great majority of the police agencies today conduct themselves in a manner that makes them a credit to law enforcement. The balance of this chapter deals with ethical areas which have given some police personnel, police administrators, and police agencies problems not only in the past, but in some cases remain present-day situations.

## THE STREET POLICEMAN

Man's struggle to maintain a society of law and order is not without many conflicts, both moral and legal. The seed of liberty is guarded daily by members of the thin blue line. One of the purposes of this chapter is to explore the ethical nature of policemen and their differences of opinions, particularly the attitudes of those dedicated, professional soldiers of law enforcement known as "street policemen," or "street cops." Few people are really aware of this basic separation within the ranks of the police service. Many carry the badge and wear the uniform, but only the dedicated are street policemen.

Moral and ethical standards vary greatly from one police agency to another. Many factors influence this, as well as the formal and informal organizational structure or hierarchy. The most important of all factors bearing a predominant role in any organization are the attitudes and moral convictions of the chief administrator. Even with this in mind, it must be remembered that he alone does not totally set the ethical climate.

Men who face tremendous danger almost daily are bonded together in a fraternity that can only be designated by the term "street policemen." Not all police officers know and feel what this term embodies. This chapter is then written to assist in advancing the rules, attitudes, and ethics that exist within this brotherhood. Many are called policemen; only the best are street policemen. Their loyalties are to principles, not men; their dialogue is different; they accept only the proven into their ranks, and they are fiercely patriotic Americans. They have always been and always will be the strongest link in law enforcement.

## TICKET FIXING

The practice of "fixing" traffic citations by police officials is an old and illegal procedure. It is usually found in communities which still have the remnants of the spoils system in their political structure. In most cases it is a symptom of a far greater underlying problem.

Some may wonder just what constitutes "fixing" a traffic citation. In substance it is any act or failure to act which permits a traffic offender to circumvent established and lawful methods of adjudication. It can take many forms, but it always involves collusion on the part of at least one branch of law enforcement.

Because some sort of forms control must be exercised, most jurisdictions have serial numbers on their citation blanks. It most cases, the records system at the court level prevents a law agency or police personnel to fail to send the original "court copy" to the courts for legal processing. If, however, the county officials are corrupt, the court records and the court officers cannot be trusted any further than the law enforcement administrators who tolerate political intervention into the process of equal justice.

The majority of individuals whose citations fail to be prosecuted seem to represent the higher social element level of the community, i.e. a sister of a councilman, a bank president, or any relative or close friend of anyone with political connections within the community. The moral crime is obvious. Law enforcement officers are sworn to uphold equal justice as a duty and not just as an ideal. No less an authority than a retired police inspector, educator, and author, Paul Weston relates that ticket fixing is not only illegal but seriously effects the morale of the police personnel. When any segment of society can violate a traffic law or any other law without fear of fine or imprisonment, the foundations of our republic are weakened.

There have been cases both past and recent to demonstrate that when discovered, the community at large will not tolerate illegal "fixing" procedures. One of the more recent experiences to demonstrate this was the mass exodus of police officials from the Orange Police Department, Orange, California, after ticket fixing was discovered in that agency. It is then the duty of the police officers and the police administrators to see that their agency does not tarnish the image of law enforcement. Those who violate this obligation often explain their positions by exclaiming that the "fix" was an extension of an "interest of justice" as they diverted the citations from the bar of justice because *they felt* that the citations were not valid. In essence, they are criminally guilty of various state and governmental codes. They are also morally guilty within the standards of the accepted law enforcement code of ethics and have performed a disservice to the honest police officers who wrote the traffic citations in good faith.

In the end, the police officer or administrator who allows this illegal and immoral practice to continue with his knowledge has also then given his consent even if he is never involved as a participating agent. In our effort for effective law enforcement there cannot be any Nuremberg excuse. Failure to act to stop a "fix" is a personal responsibility, and this obligation cannot be transferred. When ticket-fixing practices occur in a police agency, the logical person who will expose and cleanse the department will be a dedicated street police officer. This has been the case in the past; it was the case in the Orange police scandal, and it is logical to conclude that the future will also be protected by the dedicated men who cannot be bought, threatened, and thus not swayed from a duty towards principles of law and not to men who have justified graft.

There can be two effective means of eradicating this throwback of justice. The first is through the vigilance of the new breed who will not allow the past to haunt our future. The second is the possibility of a state central control of citations for all the agencies within its jurisdiction. A central control of all citations would not only prevent local politicians from interfering with the processes of law, but would also be helpful in future statistics and traffic studies on the state, county, and local levels.

## OPEN ACCOUNTS

An open account in law enforcement has many definitions and connotations. Particular reference is made to the officer who receives merchandise from a marginal establishment and upon receipt of the merchandise informs the owner or clerk to "put it on my account." This transaction is many times done with the full understanding that the merchandise is payment for some past or future extrajudicial favor that has been or will be rendered to the owner of the business.

In other words, it is simply a payoff. The term open account means just what it states — the account remains open and *unpaid*. These petty bribes can range from a package of cigarettes to a bottle of liquor. Sometimes the account is even good towards the purchase of a new car.

From a police administrative standpoint, considerable difficulty arises in the detection and prevention of such problems. There is rarely a complaining party, and less often a victim, and more remotely a sustaining witness. When it is finally discovered, it has usually grown to a proportion that a discreet discharge of the police officer or police administrator is impossible. In one way this is good, as the bribing of a police officer is a criminal matter and should be treated as such.

As a rotten apple spoils, in time, most of the basket will, and so will a police officer who is on the take. In time, others who are also morally weak will follow suit under the guidance of the initial officer who has convinced them that even in police work, double standards exist. The proverb, "God helps those who help themselves," has no place in law enforcement. The best advice that can be given to the embryo police officer is that "there is no such thing as a free lunch for a policeman."

Some examples of open accounts are as follows: A detective commander going into a local liquor store on his way home at night and picking up a bottle of whiskey on his account. The liquor store is owned directly or indirectly by a syndicate family. At the end of the month the account is balanced as no vice arrests have been made in the syndicate's establishments. Another example is an officer or patrol administrator who obtains free tires, batteries, and other parts and services from a local gas station. For his open account at the service station the owner receives a continuous patrol check at his business during the night and early morning hours. This situation creates unbalanced police protection to the detriment of other businesses in the community who do not carry open accounts for law enforcement personnel.

## BUSINESS CARDS

A business card in private industry is a necessity. It identifies the bearer as a representative of a firm and is a convenient system for recontact at a later date by the customer or client.

Professionals also know the importance of having their business cards with them at all times. In recent years the business card has evolved into many forms, sizes, and shapes in the interest of competition and artful eye appeal.

Law enforcement as a public business is one of the largest and most demanding. It is important in criminal investigations that victims and witnesses have a ready referral card at their disposal to .recontact the investigating officer should they recall something that they failed to report when the initial contact was made.

A police business card should be printed in a conservative format, usually in block or Roman type. It should include the name, address, and phone number of the police agency, and the investigating officer's name and extension number. The case number block or space should also be included. "For business purposes only" or some other indication that the business card is not to be used for any other reason than for a reference for a specific case must be clearly inscribed on the face of the card.

Because of the nature of law enforcement, there have been some instances of misuses of the police business card. There have been cases where business cards have been changed into courtesy cards by individuals whose interests were not in tune with effective law enforcement. There have been some cases where police personnel have violated public trust by writing notes on the back of their business cards and then giving them to individuals who automatically had or thought that they had some immunity from arrest or traffic citations. In effect, the inscriptions on the back of courtesy cards usually state something along the lines of "This is to introduce _____ , please extend any courtesies to him that you can." The courtesies expected are evident to any police officer who has the card handed to him in lieu of a driver's license.

Probably the majority of the courtesy cards have been altered by the persons who have received the card as a business card from police personnel. Because of this factor the police business card should have a design or blacked out reverse side to prevent alterations by either police personnel or by the citizen.

The most effective means of preventing any misuses of the police business card is through the line police officer. Under no circumstances should an officer ever honor a courtesy card.

Effective law enforcement prohibits special favors for citizens claiming to be a "friend" or relative of a fellow police officer.

## THE PURSUIT OF CRIMINALS

The pursuit of criminals and their apprehension are basic functions of law enforcement. The protection of the lives and property of the public is also not only a basic function but a sworn duty. There will be situations that will arise from time to time where these two fundamental obligations may conflict with each other. When a conflicting situation does present itself, a decision must be made by the police officer involved to determine which duty is in the best interest of the public.

An example demonstrating an area of conflicting obligations might be the evolution of a simple vehicle pursuit into a high-speed chase. An arbitrary speed or set of specific guidelines cannot be justifiably established by police administrators as to when an officer should or should not terminate a high-speed chase. This can only be determined by the individual officer involved in the situation. Only he knows the basic ingredients required to formulate a correct decision. Only he knows the exact traffic and roadway conditions, and *his ability at that time* to effectively control his police unit and apprehend the violator. It must be the individual officer, not an administrator, who should weigh the balance between the danger of the citizens on the roadway and the danger to his own safety versus the psychological danger of reoccurences should the violator escape because the police officer failed to continue pursuit.

The offender has an advantage over law enforcement personnel, as he has no responsibility to other users of the roadway except what he should morally do as a good citizen. If his freedom is paramount to him, he can set his own rules or stakes of the pursuit according to the risk he is willing to take to escape the penalty of the law. The police officer does not have this advantage. Even if he is willing to risk his life to apprehend the violator, his actions will be judged at a later date should an innocent citizen become maimed or killed as a direct result of the pursuit.

In decisions of this nature, the law enforcement officer must decide in favor of the value of the citizen's life if it is apparent that such a danger exists. Within all reason, he must, however, apprehend the violator as arbitrary "shut downs" in vehicle pursuits will result in more chases in the future by those willing to "test" the police officer or police policies.

## COMPROMISING WITH CRIMINALS

Allowing petty criminals to escape the penalty of the law for information which will lead to the arrest of a major offender has always been an ethical consideration for law enforcement officers.

By the strict interpretation of the written law any violator apprehended is expected to be brought before a court of law and be judged by either a magistrate or a jury of his peers. To allow any person to escape the legal procedure appears to be a violation of the accepted code of ethics of law enforcement, which in part states, ". . . with no compromise for crime and with relentless prosecution of criminals." Therefore, any violation of this premise would be a moral violation against the written law by which police officers are expected to live.

Unfortunately, everything is not as clear-cut or precise as many of our rules may indicate. There is also the theory of the difference between the written letter of a law and the spirit by which it should be enforced. The often-referred-to compromising with informants on minor charges must be viewed in this respect if we are to become effective in enforcing the laws of major concern to society. Surely a drug addict who is willing to disclose his source of narcotics is of less concern to the community than the apprehension and prosecution of the narcotics pusher who is responsible for the human suffering of literally hundreds of addicts.

It must be remembered that these immunities to informants are not done in the spirit of allowing someone to escape through the bars of justice, but to apprehend a greater criminal who might not have otherwise been detected. The basic question then becomes, "Do the means justify the ends?" In the interest of the protection of our communities at large, the answer appears to be obvious.

## REPORTING A FELLOW OFFICER

Through the centuries, in every walk of life, men who have informed on their peers have been held in contempt and distrust. This contempt does not limit itself to informants in criminal matters alone. How many times have we noted that the individual who informs the "boss" relative to all activities and errors of his fellow workers is soon found to be completely friendless at work. This reaction by the group is probably normal and reasonable.

In law enforcement, too, there are some police officers who spend a great deal of time and effort searching for the shortcomings of fellow officers. When this data is compiled, it is then brought to the attention of a supervisor for two purposes: The first is that the supervisor will think less of the patrolman who committed the errors. The second is that the supervisor may consider the informing patrolman rather clever, as he detected these errors and surely would not make similar mistakes. These informing police officers not only ruin their reputations but sow the seeds of distrust in the whole department. The field of law enforcement requires the closest ties between officers and distrust among brother officers can reap a fatal result.

In view of the above, it appears that the following would be a better procedure. An error committed by a patrolman should be discussed with the fellow officer who discovers the error. This discussion should be a free exchange of ideas, permitting both parties an opportunity to learn from the error. This is probably the best solution for harmony and a better quality of work performance.

For a more serious violation or error a different approach must be taken, depending, of course, on the circumstances and magnitude of the violation or error. A situation that we might explore is that of a driver under the minor influence of alcohol who turns out to be an off-duty fellow officer within your department. The first offense might be handled by informal methods. Should the situation reoccur, a field supervisor should be informed concerning the condition of the officer. Ordinary citizens who violate the safety of the roadway by driving while intoxicated are removed from the roadway. This is done for their safety as well as for the safety of the general public. The above statement does not indicate that an arrest of a fellow officer who drives while he is under the influence of alcohol is mandatory; however, disciplinary action must be taken by the supervisor if possible. If an officer completely closes his eyes to this situation and at a later date the other officer seriously injures himself or someone else as the result of driving under the influence, the fault will be shared responsibility.

In summation, the reporting of a fellow officer's petty errors to influence a supervisor is wrong and injures the reputation of both the officer who commits the error and the officer who reports it. In the end, the department also suffers because of lack of trust between its members. For a serious violation, such as driving under the influence, burglary, theft, graft, etc., the well-being of the department must be the prime consideration. Personal feelings or obedience to the outdated unwritten law that a fellow officer can do no wrong must not take precedence.

## THE TAKING OF A HUMAN LIFE

One of the most difficult decisions that a police officer can face is if and when he should take a human life. For the hardcore members of pacifist religions, the answer is simple. No human life should ever be taken under any circumstances. A police officer who subscribes to this belief should immediately seek another occupation, as his decision may well effect the life of another officer or law-abiding citizen. In essence he should be able to justify the difference between *thou shalt not murder* and the accepted translated Bible version of *thou shalt not kill.* Surely, even the Bible demonstrates time after time the justification of taking a human life under prescribed situations. Legally an officer can usually defend taking the life of an escaping felon, a suspect committing a felony, a subject about to take the life of another citizen, or attempting to kill or maim another officer or himself. Within these classifications, however, each set of circumstances should govern the actions taken.

If a felon suspect is escaping from the scene of a crime, the officer should quickly evaluate (1) the extent of the felony, i.e. is he a burglar or a murderer? (2) Can the suspect be apprehended *safely* without having to shoot him; (3) Is there *any* possibility of an innocent bystander getting shot? (4) If the suspect is a dangerous criminal, will his escape endanger the lives of fellow officers and innocent citizens?

Many pages could be written on this subject; however, the major concern rests in two areas, *the quick and the dead.* There is danger in both extremes.

The quick represents the officer who fails to evaluate a situation correctly and wrongly kills or maims in haste. His rash action will usually bring criticism against the police service, his agency, and criminal complaints against himself.

The dead are those who either failed to evaluate a situation correctly within a safe period of time, or for some reason could not bring themselves to take a human life. Among the numbers of these dead are also those good officers who depended on a fellow officer who could not face the responsibility to judge on the street level in sufficient time.

# Chapter 4

# POLICE COMMUNITY RELATIONS
## PUBLIC RELATIONS AND THE POLICE OFFICER

I N days gone by, all that was necessary to make a law enforcement officer was a body, a badge, and a beat. Today, law enforcement officers, more carefully selected, are trained in rules of evidence, techniques of arrest, scientific aids in investigations, report writing, and other important topics. One of the most important subjects in police recruit training today, and in the total field of law enforcement, is the knowledge and practical application of proper public relations.

*Webster's Dictionary* defines the public as "the general body of mankind or of a Nation, State or Community." It also defines relations as a "state of being mutually or reciprocally interested (as in social or commercial matters)." Putting these basic definitions together, the definition of public relations could be stated as, "the activities of an individual or group in building and in maintaining sound and productive relations with the public at large."

To the police officer though, public relations are based on those impressions resulting from his personal contacts and endeavors to serve his community. Viewed in this light, it is apparent that all law enforcement agencies should be concerned with public relations, and police administrators should be aware that the individual impressions made by each of their personnel is the major determinant in what the citizens of the community think about their police agency. The individual responsibilities of the police officer have become more complex and more difficult than ever before. The officer is at the center of activity and many times has to make immediate decisions. His reactions must be rapid, his reflexes sharp. He must be physically sound and mentally alert. This is the era of mob violence, militant groups, and campus disorders. The police must be quick to react in defense of justice and equality. And it must be made public knowledge that the police service is dedicated to serving the law-abiding majority as against the criminal minority. The police are neither master nor slave, but instead the line which makes the difference between an organized society and a human jungle.

## REASONS FOR PUBLIC RELATIONS

Greatest success comes through the greatest service of each department and of each man. In the European theory of law enforcement, the people are the servants of the government. Police officers are responsible only to the party in power. Public good will is not emphasized. Under the American theory, the police are the servants of the people. Service rather than domination is the rule.

If the public thinks well of its police agency or department, the majority of the citizens will offer their cooperation in matters under investigation. Another benefit is that information will be easier to obtain from interviews as the public realizes that there can be a partnership between the citizens and the police. Even those persons investigated or arrested will have respect for the abilities of law enforcement officers. Good public relations, therefore, will raise the prestige of the total police department and make police tasks easier to carry out.

Now consider another reason for good public relations: the matter of salaries, budgets, and equipment. The law enforcement community has for years been waging a battle to increase salaries. The need is urgent, and is recognized by the head of every law enforcement agency in the country. Many agencies have partially succeeded in achieving higher salaries. The sad part of it is that in many areas law enforcement officers, because of the lack of good public relations, have not been able to impress this need upon the citizens.

Not only is there a problem of low wages for police personnel, but in many areas police budgets also are not adequate. Training programs suffer from lack of funds, and law enforcement officers have to operate with old, outmoded, and sometimes dangerously defective equipment. Many law enforcement agencies are experiencing difficulty in attracting the type of personnel they desire because of low salaries and obvious inadequate equipment problems.

Law enforcement officers must recognize that it does little or no good to complain to each other and to offer mutual sympathy. They must realize that through better public relations they can achieve the improvement in law enforcement they desire.

The citizens of the community are the policeman's employers. They, like all other employers, expect efficient service and want pleasant contacts with their employees. Like all other employers they will regard good service and pleasant contacts with interest and support.

It is imperative that law enforcement officers abide by the previously mentioned ground rules of public relations. It must be remembered that the police are the first line of defense, and the public must have the utmost confidence in them. Also, efficient, effective work and good public relations are the tools that can effect any major improvements.

## VALUE OF GOOD PUBLIC RELATIONS

The International Association of Chiefs of Police state that the most important phase of public relations work is the contact made by the officer during the course of the day's work. This would include the sum total of all contacts, attitudes, impressions, and opinions which constitute the relation of the public to the police department.

The success of a good police officer is measured in a large part by the assistance rendered to him by law-abiding citizens. Desire to assist the police is usually dormantly present in the average citizen. To kindle that desire into action is the job of policemen.

Ignorance is the parent of suspicion, and information is a basis of understanding. The police must keep the public informed in order to combat crime more efficiently. The police must also be aware of the needs of the public. If a police agency can effectively satisfy its public it is planting the seeds of good will which will eventually assist that agency in the short- and long-range goals or objectives.

In discussing the values of good public relations we must also consider the police-community relations division and the individual entrusted with this complex and challenging position. This person can either nurture this problem and obtain good will for the agency or demolish the whole public relations program.

Selection of this individual should be careful and deliberate. He should possess certain qualifications above those of the average officer. Categories of qualifications should include an excellent education, a good moral character, a high intelligence, a healthy attitude, a good presentable appearance, and the knowledge of the importance of courtesy. They must be officers who are respected and trusted by the other men in the department.

The training of the men assigned to public relations should be continuous. They should be aware of all the current events in the city that might affect the program.

## CONDUCT

Impressions based on personal contacts are most important tools of the law enforcement officer. The citizen's impressions of an officer will determine to a large extent what he thinks of all law enforcement personnel. Each officer is a symbol of all law enforcement.

William M. Evarts once said, "There is nothing great in the world but man, and there is nothing great in man but character."

Conduct has many ramifications. Here listed below are a few that deserve mentioning:

1. *Attitude* — does the officer want to make a good impression?

2. *Courtesy* — The essence of public relations; a quality most desired of police officers, according to surveys.

3. *Cooperation* — a part of good conduct essential phase of life. J. Edgar Hoover, director, Federal Bureau of Investigation, has said, "In the discharge of duties as sacred as those of a law enforcement officer, there can be no excuse for lack of cooperation, petty jealousy, or bickering."

4. *Community spirit* — participation in community functions is an excellent media to create good will. The uniform of the officer does not diminish the need for community spirit but

increases it.

5. *Church activity* — will tend to enhance character.

6. *Character, morals, and personal conduct* — a policeman lives in a goldfish bowl. He must exemplify the model citizen on his off-duty hours as well as those on duty.

7. *Salesmanship* — over 70 percent of all complaints against officers result from the officer's not selling himself. A good salesman is also a good listener.

8. *Appearance* — dress, hair, shoes, and uniform must be neat at all times. The public will judge the officer and his department to a large extent by the individual appearance of the officer.

9. *Relations* — good relations within the police department are necessary as the personnel have to be sold on the department in order to sell it to others.

10. *Community spirit or services* — services beyond the normal call of duty cements public relations.

    a. Checking homes when people are on vacation.

    b. Organizing youth groups.

    c. Safety patrols.

    d. Building police camps to be used by the public.

11. *Efficiency of operations* — efficiency is accomplishing a task in the shortest time possible with the least amount of effort. The characteristic of success as Thomas Edison once said, "is accomplished by one percent inspiration and 99 percent perspiration."

12. *Good administration* — administrative ability is not born in a man, it is developed. Without good administration where men are treated fairly but firmly, suggestions, are encouraged and skills are acknowledged, the department cannot advance and new administrators cannot be developed. Disgruntled men mean no public relations.

## COMMUNICATING WITH PUBLIC AND
## BUILDING PUBLIC RELATIONS

Realizing that public relations is a two-way street, the community must develop an understanding of the police function and of the problems that confront the police, as well as the realization that communication is the tool needed to achieve this rapport.

This rapport must come in the form of a free channel of communication in which each side recognizes the other's faults and sympathizes with the other's problems. The people, and through them their local governments, must recognize that police departments require the finest up-to-date equipment; that they must be adequately manned; that police officers should receive more extensive education, not merely in basic police techniques, but in legal issues, social questions, and psychology; and that police salaries must be increased to attract and keep high-quality men in police work.

The initative for developing this understanding rests in large part with the police personnel. This is because police departments are well-organized, structured units and, more important, because they are public servants. Speaking on urban riots, Warren Christopher, Deputy U. S. Attorney General, made a point which is applicable to the entire range of police relations when he said, "Society will depend heavily on already overworked, woefully underpaid policemen. Whether a routine arrest may become the spark for a conflagration will so often depend on the quality of the man with the badge."

It must be remembered that it is the communicator's responsibility to be understood. This obligation is the great challenge that faces law enforcement and those who are a part of it. Everyone from the recruit to the chief of police is responsible for the public relations job of restoring confidence in law enforcement and the department he represents. This is a vital requirement in the acceptance of law and order by the public, but this is not the only answer. The prosecutors, the courts, and the supreme court have an equal, if not greater responsibility; and the actions of some of these in recent years have not been encouraging.

Police departments, prosecutors, and our courts have an important role in working together to build the confidence of our people in law and order and justice. There is great room for improvement in effective communication in these areas, but communication must also be reflected in actions.

Understanding is the basis for solving man's problems. Communication can play a vital role in reaching that understanding. Its implementation can be of great value to every police department and court in the land. Effective communication can lead to understanding. We must remember if the police do not understand what the police need, they are not likely to support departmental requests.

## THE ST. LOUIS MISSOURI POLICE-COMMUNITY RELATIONS PROGRAM

Let us now explore the efforts that the St. Louis police department is extending in the police community relations area. The city of St. Louis is a large, metropolitan city with diversified industry. It has a population of 3,000,000 people including its suburbs. Of this number, there are 1,200,000 Negroes, as well as other small minority groups. The St. Louis Police Department's public relations program has been given national recognition as one of the most comprehensive and finest in the nation. The police community relations division has staff members assigned to each district of the city. It operates seven storefront centers and conducts many programs designed to create better support between citizens and police. A commissioned and civilian staff of twenty-five is assigned to police community relations.

### Adult Programs

#### St. Louis Council on P-CR

This council, an outgrowth of the committee established in 1955 by the National Conference of Christians and Jews, is composed of civic leaders from all segments of society and meets regularly with the Board of Police Commissioners, Chief of Police, and P-CR Division Staff. Its function is to advise on the general status of police-community relations in St. Louis and on specific P-CR programs.

#### P-CR District Committees

The heart of the entire P-CR program is a citizen committee in each of the nine police districts. These committees now have a combined membership of more than 7,000 citizens who meet monthly to discuss problems confronting police and citizens and usually see a program on some phase of law enforcement. Each committee has four subcommittees: law enforcement, juveniles, sanitation, and businessmen's, which carry out specific P-CR projects such as those listed in the following section.

## P-CR Committees in Housing Developments

In police districts where public housing projects are located, the district committee has been encouraged to hold special meetings in the projects so that more residents will attend. From this, separate committees have been formed in Pruitt-Igoe, Carr Square-Vaughn, and Darst-Webbs.

## Businessmen's Committees

Committees are established especially for businessmen and women in each district since they have special problems. Eight of the nine districts now have regularly scheduled businessmen committee meetings as well as the monthly membership meetings.

## P-CR District Officers

In eight of the nine police districts, officers assigned to that district were selected to devote full time to police-community relations. It is their responsibility to establish support with all groups and organizations within their district. Districts 3, 4, 7, 8, and 9 have two P-CR officers each, while 2, 5, and 6, have one per district.

## District P-CR Storefront Centers

These centers, usually located in vacant stores, are in the third, fourth, seventh, eighth, and ninth districts. They serve as offices for the district P-CR officers and headquarters for the district committees, as well as a place other than a police station where citizens can discuss their problems with an officer. The district commander and district juvenile and sanitation officers keep regular hours at the centers. Two centers are now open sixteen hours daily.

## Communications Program

In order to establish open channels of communication with all segments of society, the Board of Police Commissioners, Chief of Police, and P-CR personnel meet regularly with civil rights leaders in St. Louis. Meetings are also held with representatives of the Urban League, Human Development Corporation, and other community organizations to develop areas of cooperation.

## Mass Media Relations

Through newpapers, radio, and television, a constant effort is made to keep the citizens of St. Louis informed about departmental policies, procedures, and innovations and P-CR activities. Representatives of the mass media meet once a year with the board of police commissioners and the chief of police to exchange information and discuss common approaches to the problems of the community.

## Speakers Bureau

Speakers and films on many police topics are available free from the St. Louis police department for civic, church, school, and other organizations. Police experts make the presentations on a large list of subjects.

## Youth Programs

### P-CR Youth Council

A P-CR youth council is coordinated by the division. Each high school principal is asked to assign a member from each class and the school newspaper to be a member of the council which will meet monthly at police headquarters. This council will serve as liaison with the schools.

*Headstart Program*

Officers visit each headstart program in the city as frequently as possible to teach pedestrian safety.

*School Visitation*

Officers visit each elementary school in the city to provide a school program. Films are purchased for this purpose. This program is coordinated with the board of education, which prepares the schedule. The trafficopter also visits these schools as frequently as possible.

District P-CR officers also teach the section on the police department in the "We Elect" eighth-grade civics program in the St. Louis public schools. The "We Elect" schedule for P-CR officers is coordinated in the P-CR office.

*Say Hi Program*

Say hi cards are printed for distribution to elementary school students by district officers and staff officers. Youngsters are encouraged to wave and say hello to officers in this program.

*Youth Activities*

Staff members conduct a variety of juvenile programs including neighborhood dances with the police bus and its amplification equipment. Youngsters are taken to ball games and other activities such as movies and entertainment shows by division officers.

*Prenatal Program*

Officers conduct programs for expectant parents, informing them of the need for proper education of children in their attitudes toward police.

*Special Youth Program*

An officer works during the football off-season with hardcore youth in the high crime districts by visiting taverns, pool halls, and other hangouts. He is also active in the high schools.

### Explorer Post

The division staff forms an Explorer Post whose specialty interest is law enforcement.

### Police-Junior Aid Program

This program, jointly sponsored by police and Y.M.C.A. is coordinated by the division staff although carried out in the districts. It included in 1968 about ninety-eight fourteen- and fifteen-year-olds.

### Cruiser Tours

The division coordinates with the juvenile committees the cruiser tours, outlined under district programs. Other organizations are given cruiser tours when manpower permits.

### P-CR Award

Each spring, the division establishes a ceremony whereby the police board presents a framed letter of thanks to each active member of the executive committees in the nine districts.

In the fall, the division arranges for the presentation of a letter of thanks to citizens who have contributed to the success of the P-CR program.

### Clergy-Police Program

The division has initiated and is coordinator of a program designed to improve communications and understanding between police and the clergy.

### P-CR Film

The division is responsible for coordinating a thirty-minute film on police-community relations, being produced by a local film company.

## Combined Programs

### Patrol Area Leader Plan

In each of the 108 patrol areas in the city, a citizen leader has been chosen from among the membership of the district committees. These leaders are responsible for recruiting members for the committee and carrying out the committee's P-CR programs in that area. They meet weekly with the sergeant who supervises the area to discuss the crime situation and other neighborhood problems.

### Citizens Against Crime

More than 600,000 Citizens Against Crime cards, which request that citizens call police if they see a crime committed or a suspicious person, automobile, or incident, have been distributed to citizens of St. Louis during the past three years. This type of program has been initiated in cities throughout the country and has assisted not only in police-community relations but also in the reduction of criminal activities.

### Law Enforcement Assistance Award

Every three months the district committee chairman and the district commander select one or more citizens whom they feel have an outstanding contribution to law enforcement in their district during the previous three months. From these nominations, the board of police commissioners names the winner of the law enforcement assistance award and presents a plaque to the winner and certificates of appreciation to the nominees in a special ceremony at police headquarters.

### Block Watchers

Citizens who remain at home during the day are assigned certain times during which they watch for suspicious persons, automobiles, or incidents on their block and report them to police.

### Law Enforcement Day

During law enforcement month, which is May of each year, the division holds a special open house and programs for interested citizens. As many as 15,000 citizens attend the open house.

### Burglary Survey

Members of the businessmen's subcommittee contact business-men in the district, informing them that upon request a district detective will make a survey of their premises, pointing out weak spots in their security system which might encourage a burglary or other crime.

### Sanitation Program

An ongoing program to improve sanitation conditions in the district is carried out by the sanitation subcommittee through cooperation with other neighborhood organizations and distribu-tion of sanitation literature.

### Whom to Call

Since a large number of calls for service received by the St. Louis Police Department do not deal with police matters, the P-CR division has prepared and distributes a list of the correct city agency to call for various problems.

### Mock Trial

In order to give high school students an opportunity to see how a criminal trial is conducted, the district committee sponsors a mock trial in each high school during the year, using local university law students as advisors and lawyers, and high school students as witnesses and jurors.

## Block Homes

The district committee encourages and provides guidance and assistance to any PTA or Mother's Club that wants to start a Block Home Program. Mothers who will be home when children are going and coming from school place a "Block Home" sign in their front window, and children are instructed that they can take refuge in these homes if they become frightened, sick, or injured.

## Success

Each spring the P-CR division presents to the most outstanding chairman, subcommittee chairman, and individual members from the nine district committees.

## HOW EVERY OFFICER IS AFFECTED

### Police-Community Relations Programs Within the Department

### Recruit Training

During their sixteen weeks of training in the Police Academy, all police recruits take a three-hour course in Human Relations. Taught by sociologists and psychologists from local colleges and universities, the course includes instruction on such topics as human behavior, the psychology of prejudice, American culture, and social disorganization. Recently, ten hours of field trips led by a social worker have been added to acquaint new officers with the socioeconomic conditions of the city. Recruits also receive instruction in the mechanics of the police-community relations program and mass media relations, taught by members of the P-CR Division. Refresher courses in human relations and P-CR are included once a year in the in-service training required of all officers.

All recruits are now being assigned for one day on a one-to-one basis with a P-CR officer operating a Storefront Center. The recruits are introduced to the neighborhood and its residents so they can gain a better understanding of the problems of the residents.

*Sergeants Program*

A sergeant from each district spends three days learning about the P-CR program. They spend this time working with the district P-CR officers.

## HOW THE COMMUNITY IS AFFECTED

### The End Result of Police-Community Relations Programs

After studying the above police-community relations program of a large metropolitan city, what conclusions can be reached? Does a program like this "pay" for itself? The answer is yes.

Police-community relations programs pay dividends to both the police and the citizen. It cannot be measured in monetary value, but it has assisted in creating understanding between the police and the public. The police function of any society is a service to that society. There must be a mutual respect from both officer and citizen for each other if the police public relations program in any city is to be effective – the officer's realizing his daily responsibilities to the citizen on his beat and the citizen's understanding what the officer must do to uphold law and order.

The American way of life of equal opportunity for all who will help themselves is on the threshold of realization. Law enforcement stands in the vanguard as a bulwark, preserving the peace and protecting the lives and property of all its citizens.

# Chapter 5

# POLICE UNIONS

 $T$ ODAY, the law enforcement community is again faced with one of its greatest historical problems which will reoccur from time to time. It is the question of whether or not police officers should form a national police union and affiliate with a national labor organization. This is a question that has to be decided on its merits and not on whether unions are basically good or bad. If a national police union can assist the police service in obtaining just benefits and help to achieve some of its professional goals, then the idea of unionization must be seriously considered. However, if it cannot accomplish the goals of the law enforcement community, it will amount to nothing more than just another dues-charging organization for police personnel.

## HISTORICAL ASPECTS

The local unionization of police departments started at the turn of the century. This was the period of our nation's history when the frontiers had recently been settled and the metropolitan centers and urban areas were beginning their growth. This population increase demanded the expansion of existing police agencies and the formation of additional ones to insure adequate protection of the lives and property of its citizens.

As police departments increased in size, the line beat police officers became more and more removed from their administrators. To help bridge this gap in communications between line and administration, local fraternal, social, and benevolent police organizations were formed. These organizations soon became the spokesmen for police personnel in dealing with such matters as conditions of employment. They were encouraged by administrators and recognized as a valuable morale factor by the departments.

During this period, there was cause for the average policeman to be dissatisfied with his conditions of employment, and undoubtedly the promises of union organizers fell on receptive ears. The time was ripe for unionization, but one police union almost killed the idea of police unionization forever.

## The Boston Police Strike

This event occurred on September 9, 1919 in Boston, Massachusetts, and was known as the Boston Police Strike. This strike was to set the public against police unions, to cause anti-union police legislation, and to assist a governor in becoming President of the United States.

The foundation for the strike was laid in the early fall when the Boston union requested permission from the Boston Police Commissioner to affiliate with the American Federation of Labor. The situation reached its climax on the ninth, when the Commissioner refused to sanction affiliation and also suspended some police officers for union activities. On the same day, the union counteracted by voting to strike and 12,000 men walked off their posts. There had been few preparations made in the event of a strike, and the city of Boston suddenly found itself without police protection.

What happened next was best described by an unknown witness: "Little groups of irresponsible hoodlums commenced their pranks. Soon the more venturesome began removing spare tires from cars and knocking off the hats of pedestrians . . . . A trolley car was held up and stoned by a mob, and the passengers were forcibly ejected. Rapidly what had been a vague spirit of mischief . . . turned into rioting. Windows were smashed in stores, and the goods were seized, fruit stands were overturned, and the primitive instinct to destroy was let loose (1)."

The following day, at the request of Boston Mayor Andrew J. Peters, Governor Calvin Coolidge sent the State Guard to restore order. Before order was finally restored, at least eight people were dead, nearly a hundred were injured, and over a million dollars of

1. Judge Irving B. Zeichner, "Police Unions," *Law and Order* (New York, April, 1959), p. 16.

property had been destroyed.

"There is no right to strike against the public safety by anybody, anywhere, anytime." This statement, issued by Governor Coolidge at the time of the strike, describes the mood of the nation during the 1920's and '30's. President Wilson, in a vigorous statement supporting Governor Coolidge, expressed the national view of the police function. He stated, "A strike of policemen of a great city, leaving that city at the mercy of an army of thugs, is a crime against civilization. In my judgment the obligation of a policeman is as sacred and direct as the obligation of a soldier. He is a public servant, not a private employee, and the whole honor of the community is in his hands. He has no right to prefer any private advantage to public safety." This concept still expresses the national view. Soon after the Boston strike and these statements, many city and state governments, by ordinance and legislation, moved to bar not only police unions but also possible future strikes. The legislative mood was established: "Policemen cannot strike."

### The 1940-1950 Era

It was not until the 1940's that local police unions began to appear. Slowly through the forties and fifties more police departments began to organize unions. In 1956, a survey conducted by the International Association of Chiefs of Police (IACP) showed that 44 unions were in operation, of which 41 were affiliated with AFL and 3 with CIO. No information was available on the number that had formed and then later disbanded.

Again in 1959, unionization of police was projected on the front pages of the newspapers. This time, James R. Hoffa's International Brotherhood of Teamsters attempted to affiliate with the New York City Police Department. Before the attempt failed, because of public opinion, the teamsters had set up picket lines around police headquarters.

A survey conducted during this period, by IACP, showed that the average policeman was dissatisfied with his conditions of employment, wages, working hours, pensions, and other benefits. However, it concluded that "union membership was contrary to the basic nature of police duties" (2). It therefore appears that the trend against police unionization had not changed in forty years.

## Present-day Aspects

Today, however, the public is again viewing the police with a "jaundiced eye," watching the police reject or support established practices. Indirect strike forms are being attempted by some police groups. In an effort to embarrass elected officials, they are picketing and protesting with parades and rallies during off-duty time in front of city halls. Other indirect strike forms are used while on duty and are called blue flu, ticket blizzards, and ticket slow-downs.

The police officers participating in these demonstrations and behaving in such an unorthodox manner certainly do not improve public relations or public confidence. Intimidating the public by slow-downs and blue flue is unpopular with most officers and is done reluctantly. Most men in police work are dedicated, but dedication is not negotiable, and these unethical means, used to increase wages, are acts of desperation (3). The public has become more aware of the policeman's situation. The factors that probably helped most were the increase of organized crime, the frequent demonstrations and riots, and not the informal strike methods. The public is demanding more of the police now than ever before.

## Legislative Aids

One of the first states to help the police officer was Pennsylvania. Its legislature passed a constitutional amendment which provides for compulsory arbitration. This amendment states that policemen have "either through labor organizations or other representatives designated by 50 percent of the officers in a department, the right to bargain collectively with their public employers concerning the terms and conditions of the

2. *Ibid.,* p. 26.
3. Sgt. Floyd M. Neoling, "The Police Pay Problem: A Solution," *Law and Order* (New York, October, 1969), p. 18.

employment. This includes compensation, hours, working conditions, retirement, pensions, and other benefits, and in the event the law-making body does not approve the agreement reached by collective bargaining, then either party to the dispute may request the appointment of a board of arbitration" (4).

Other states are following Pennsylvania in passing this type of legislation, and other states are studying and considering such laws. This type of legislation can, without a doubt, assist the policeman in obtaining not only a better standard of living but also more security.

## The Most Recent Attempts

Again, the fire has been lit, but this time on a larger scale. On September 16, 1969, a meeting was held in Washington, D.C. for the purpose of establishing a national police union affiliated with the A.F.L./C.I.O. Attending this meeting were delegates from eight police departments throughout the country. They selected a chairman and set the date of November 1, 1969, for drafting and adopting the constitution and bylaws for this proposed union. It must be noted that the A.F.L./C.I.O. stated that it would not accept this union if it includes a strike clause in its constitution. On November 1 and 2, the delegates met in Omaha, Nebraska, and, in closed session, performed their task.

How this union will operate is only known to a few at this time. Basically, the national union would be accepted by the A.F.L./C.I.O. and then grant charters to local police agencies wishing to join. Within this charter, there would be a "no strike clause," and the right by the member to carry on independent negotiations with his employer. This would infer that the national union would only provide moral support and general guidance to the local.

Some of the benefits and objectives of the union, as taken from their draft constitution, are summarized as follows:

1. To promote the organization of workers in general, and police officers in particular.

---

4. Harry W. More, "The Era of Police Collective Bargaining," *Law and Order* (New York, June, 1969), p. 22.

2. To promote the welfare of the membership and to provide a voice in the determination of the terms and conditions of employment. The union is committed to the process of collective bargaining as the most desirable, democratic, and effective method to achieve results.

3. To employ available legislative and political measures to obtain this action.

4. To promote civil service legislation and career service in government.

5. To provide research and educational services and activities designed to assist members and affiliates.

6. To foster cooperation among affiliated police officers.

7. To cooperate with other labor organizations in particular, and other segments of our society in general, towards the end that the material wealth of American society be more justly distributed, and the moral promise of American ideals be realized.

It is expected by the writers of the constitution that when these objectives take effect under the new union, they will have a great effect upon the morale and efficiency of the police community.

The new proposed union has prohibited the main element most people are afraid of – the strike. However, those against such a union still use this item as fuel to strengthen their argument. They claim that the "no strike" clause is an admission of the incapacity of the union to assist the police service in solving its grievances. The strike factor has always been the "hammer" or power behind unionization. Without this power the union provides no additional advantages to the police community. It is because of this that many of the police personnel feel that joining the union would only result in a waste of time and money.

Nonsupporters of the idea of unionization argue that a union will hinder law enforcement in its attempt to become professionalized to any degree. The term "union," as understood by the majority of the people, implies a technical skill or occupation instead of a profession such as medicine or law.

## SUMMARY

History has demonstrated that attempts to unionize law

enforcement has usually created nothing but additional problems for the police service. The earlier attempts at unionization have created a distasteful image of what could happen again should police personnel consider a national police union.

Another item which may be of concern is the "no strike" clause. Does the "no strike" clause *guarantee* that the national police union will not change its policy in the future? Some state that the union members will enforce this clause, but the honor system has not been sufficient in stopping cases of the "blue flu." The strike has always been the tool of labor unions, and there is no reason to believe it will not continue to be. It appears that the "no strike" clause is only a face-saving device for the union should its members strike.

Unions also are notorious for interfering in the affairs of the administrative processes. A clear example of such interference was displayed in Omaha on December 1, 1969. At that time, the police chief put out a directive on the off-duty wearing of the uniform. The local Omaha Police Union immediately challenged this directive as affecting off-duty employment. Many of the officers had off-duty security positions which included their wearing regular official police uniforms. The union stated that it was looking after the welfare of the men, but the welfare in question was the right of union members to use an official uniform for personal gain. This type of action turns the union into "watch dogs" of administrative actions, dealing with more than employee/employer relationship. It is felt that there are already sufficient legally constituted bodies performing this job.

The right to collective bargaining does not require a union to make it work under the new laws. According to the laws that have been written thus far, the policemen only need representatives to bargain for them. They do not specify that a union has to do the bargaining, so if a department does not have a fraternal organization, any pro-police oriented individual from the community could take the policeman's case to the city council and on to an arbitration board. This law has two results. First, it gives more power to existing organizations, and secondly, it saves the policeman money by not requiring additional membership in a new organization.

It is also felt that affiliation with a national labor organization could possibly lead to conflicting loyalties. This would really be obvious in the case of a brother union picketing, and union police officers stationed in the immediate area trying to preserve order. Picketing is another major tool of the union because other unions are expected to respect the picket line. Where will the policeman stand? Will he perform his job or remain true to his union? He cannot possibly fulfill both obligations.

We can anticipate problems in police departments with a union which some officers refuse to join. The nonmember, for one reason or another, does not join, but yet he still receives all the benefits that the union might bring about. This more than likely will cause friction between the non-union man and the union member. Since a police department cannot be a closed shop, pressure will probably be brought on the non-union man to join, thereby causing conflict within the department.

It is therefore felt that unionization can in no way benefit the law enforcement community. Since the awakening of the great masses of the American population to the need for good, efficient law enforcement, the police service cannot help but to receive better future benefits. Granted, the road for progress has been a difficult one, and the benefits that have been gained thus far have not been through implied force or through threats of establishing a national police union. Police personnel have already organized and established many noteworthy police associations which can and will take advantage of bargaining legislation for its members. Not only will the existing police fraternal orders assist law enforcement achieve its goals, but they can do so without injuring the police image.

In essence, the police community does not need the problems that unionization can and will bring; it has enough problems to cope with already.

# Chapter 6

# A NATIONAL POLICE FORCE

A WIDELY discussed topic within the law enforcement community for a number of years has been the possibility of the creation of a national police force. There are many factors which indicate the advisability of a centralized uniformed law enforcement agency. There are also, however, other factors which may indicate the danger of such a concept.

## ADVANTAGES

### Uniformity

One of the major advantages pointed out by the advocates of the National Police Force concept is that there would be uniformity which would make the task of law enforcement much more efficient. Procedures and policies could be established which would be standardized throughout the national system. In this way each man would know his job and what is expected of him no matter where he was assigned.

### Recruitment

One of the major problems confronting the majority of our cities is the recruitment of qualified police personnel. Our present system is a competitive effort between law enforcement agencies which finds the most desirable men seeking employment where the best offers are advertised. Unfortunately, many cities and counties can not compete with their wealthier counterparts. A result of this many times makes the difference between richer, larger cities having the best applicants and the poorer communities being forced to select among unfit candidates. Some agencies find themselves without applicants at all.

As a national recruitment effort all areas of the country could be given equal priority as there would be no competition among police agencies, but just among the applicants who would like to become police officers.

## Uniforms

Traveling across our nation one could note the many different police uniforms and patrol cruisers. Many studies have been made to show the relationship between the various uniforms and public attitudes. Basically the blue-black meets more public resentment than the tan issues. Recent opinions of some indicate that a blazer-type jacket and slacks create the best public image. This may be true; however, the idea of changing police officers from easily identified representatives of the law to unidentified individuals may not be desirable.

The one fact that is obvious is that the more variations of police uniforms that exist, the more confusion will exist among the general public. Another factor to be concerned with might be the cost or price difference between a purchase of one uniform model for a total national police force and the purchase of different uniforms for all the different-sized law enforcement agencies. The same reasoning might also be applied to the purchase of police cruisers, weapons, and other needed material.

## Salary Structure and Retirement

In our present system of local, county, and state uniformed law enforcement, one can note the great range of salary and retirement differences. Depending on where an interested law enforcement candidate applies, he can expect to be paid a salary from slightly in excess of $200 a month to $1,000 a month. He may also retire in some agencies after twenty years of active service or have to work until a certain age is attained. The usual age retirement is fifty-five years of age. Retirement varies from twenty to thirty-four years of active service for the twenty-one-year-old rookie police officer, depending on which agency he joins.

In a national police structure naturally a uniform system could be established. This uniform system could also guarantee equal recognition and wages for service throughout our republic for all law enforcement personnel.

## Duplication of Efforts

The system of independent police agencies ranging from state to local control does present many problems in duplication of effort. Many states have found it advantageous to have a central criminal laboratory instead of each agency's attempting to create its own experts.

Many communities experience the frustration of locating police authority and responsibility. Cities are severed into partial county areas and irregular city boundaries. The citizens are often required to remember which police agency to call depending on what side of the street their residence is located. Some streets, even though they are in the center of the city, may not be incorporated. If this is the case, a county sheriff's patrol unit or a state patrol cruiser might have to travel several miles to answer the citizen's request for service. The more vital the requirement for police assistance, the more obvious the problem becomes (see Fig. 1).

Naturally a unified national police force would have no boundary limitations. The citizen would only have to know the police phone number for his area, being assured that the closest police unit will be dispatched to assist him. Patrol areas could be established on a bases of called-for services and enforcement needs instead of political boundaries.

## Ability to Transfer

When a police officer presently leaves the service of one police agency for that of another, he usually loses not only his seniority, but his retirement time as well. There have been cases of police personnel having to virtually lose their life's efforts for law enforcement because of a needed move for family health purposes. State patrol officers have the advantage of transferring anywhere within a state as long as there is an opening where the officer would like to transfer and that he is the senior officer making the

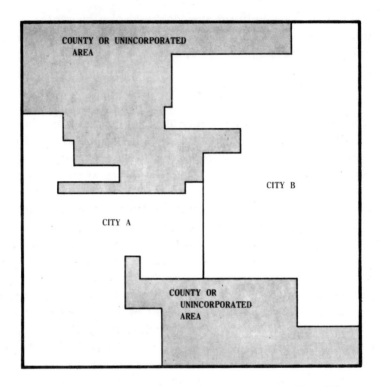

Figure 1. The possible boundries that may separate two cities with county or unincorporated areas.

request. With a national police force this system would merely be extended from state to national maneuverability.

### Freedom from Local Politics

The power of local politicians to rule law enforcement is a definite problem within our present system. Many times the biggest criminals with a city are the so-called pillars of the community. The nameless wandering drunk is taken to jail without a second thought. Those drunks with the *right* influence may obtain service from a radio call message to have a relative pick up the individual or to a free ride home. This type of influence is, of course, adverse to our sworn duties and damages police-public relations. The bulk of a community is represented by the average citizen without political connections who rightly feels that the law should be enforced impartially. When it is not enforced impartially, the fault rests with the police.

Realistically the degree of favoritism is usually issued from the chief of police. He is in an awkward situation as he is ususally not protected by a civil service system or by any other means of job security. He therefore must rely on those who have the power to hire and fire the various city department heads – the city manager, the mayor, and the city council. Many times other power structures exist which must also be recognized and dealt with.

State patrols have found an advantage over metropolitan police agencies as they are able to impartially arrest without fear of a city or county power structure. Nationally, this advantage would be raised to the point of impartial enforcement without fear of state officials' ability to interfere as well.

## DISADVANTAGES

### Difficulties in Establishing a National Police Force

With the many advantages of such a system the main problem would be how to set up the force. The great majority of city, county, and state officials certainly would not willingly give up their political arrest immunity and authority. Local chiefs of police may prefer to be administrators of smaller departments rather than gamble with an uncertain future. Of course, the exceptionally qualified police administrators would realize that their future would be almost unlimited as compared to their current ability to assert their knowledge and influence in law enforcement.

### Who Would Administer the Force?

One important question would be who would be responsible for the administration of such a powerful agency. An individual such as J. Edgar Hoover is a once in a lifetime gift to our community.

A political aspect then arises as to who chooses the top administrator. Naturally a political obligation on the part of the chief of the agency would only be a magnification of local powers over local chiefs. The answer might lie in the establishment of a police board or commission partially elected and partially selected. Also a term limitation must be imposed so not as to create another federal entity such as the Supreme Court where once appointed, only death or resignation seems to be the answer to incompetence or senility. A high law enforcement position is no place for a man reaching senility even though once useful and alert.

## Centralized Power

There is a basic concern on the part of many Americans about federalized power. The fundamental fear which would concern most citizens would probably be the gestapo power image that would project itself too much. Constitutional conservatives might project a possible take-over from elements of the Left. Their feelings may be more justified, as with a multiple of law enforcement agencies no political structure controls the entire law enforcement community.

Even the military structure in America is separated so that not too much power is placed in the hands of a few. When a few are able to exert exceptional authority, the fear of infiltration and possible adoption of policies which are not in the best interest of the nation is reasonable. Again the Supreme Court might be cited as an example of what could happen on an executive level.

# Chapter 7

# POLICE REVIEW BOARDS

THE right of a specialized occupation to police and regulate itself is fundamental. Law enforcement agencies and their personnel are subject to review constantly. Municipal police departments, particularly, are under the daily scrutinizing eye of many, i.e. the Federal Bureau of Investigation, the District Attorney's Office, the Attorney General's Office, the Grand Jury, the City Attorney, the City Council, the Courts, the Civil Service Commission, and the Internal Affairs Division of the agency itself. No other occupation or profession is subject to such close observation and prompt criticism by so many entities. In no other occupation or profession is it a crime not to report a criminal offense committed by one of its members, no matter how minor the offense may be.

Within the last few years there has been an accelerated effort on the part of certain individuals and organizations to create still another entity to monitor the activities of police personnel. Although many names have been used to describe the various citizen groups and "Blue Ribbon" committees, the basic idea is the creation of a citizen-police review board.

## WHAT IS A REVIEW BOARD?

Let us first examine what a "police review board" is in the general frame of reference as advocated by the misguided, poorly informed, and sometimes well meaning "Liberal" elements of our society. Unfortunately the same basic description also fits that type of board or committee as advocated by the radical Left elements who are the loudest voices calling for the total destruction of our American republic and way of life by any means, legal or illegal.

The Liberals presuppose that if a group of lay citizens or

Figure 2. The role of a civilian review board and who constitutes membership on such a board.

nonpolice experts were to have the power to investigate and monitor the activities of police agencies and their personnel, greater assurances of individual liberty would follow. The radical Left advocates this same formation of untrained citizens to "watch" the police, as this creation would partially paralyze the police into a state of inactivity, thereby permitting greater abuses of the law by these revolutionaries.

Many of our citizens really do not realize just what constitutes a police review board. It is difficult to be for or against an idea unless a clear understanding exists in someone's mind on just what it is. Unfortunately there are about as many descriptions of what constitutes a police review board as there are names for it.

Basically the board is supposed to be a group of citizens who would have the power to investigate anything irregular concerning police matters. In some areas they also set the penalty should they find that in their opinion a police officer was at fault. The idea of untrained people deciding the fate of trained specialists is as valid in the law enforcement field as it would be in the medical or legal profession.

One fact has been borne out concerning these boards. In every city that they have been established, the results have been detrimental to police morale and effectiveness. Perhaps this is just what it is supposed to accomplish.

## WHO ARE APPOINTED?

Another area of vagueness concerning the formation of a police review board is how the members are selected, and if they are appointed, who has the authority to appoint candidates. Most of the few police review boards that are still in existence are composed of representatives of minority and community groups who claim to represent the downtrodden citizens. The vast majority of these so-called representatives of the "discriminated class" are naturally predisposed to an anti-police attitude. They are in effect practicing the old Jim Crow law in reverse – the police officer is guilty regardless of the evidence. This atmosphere of predetermined guilt is one of the main objections of law enforcement personnel throughout our nation, and its foundations are built on solid facts supported by the history of this newer creation.

## POLICE ATTITUDES

Most police personnel appropriately believe that a civilian police review board is nothing less than a "witch hunt," and not an honest attempt in any stretch of the imagination for a search for the truth. Policemen know that any legitimate search for truth in the police situation requires highly trained investigators and unbiased judges. A civilian police review board usually, if ever, has neither.

Policemen as an occupational group are adamantly opposed to review boards, and it is easy to understand their reasoning. No group enjoys the creation of a third party to monitor their activities when in fact the third party has no training to make the proper decisions. No group enjoys a third party soliciting complaints about its members. The ranks of the police community feel that the civilian review board is a political parasite with no real creative objective.

Many times a policeman is required, often with no more than a few seconds, to decide on a course of action. Years later in the highest court, educated men of the law vote 5 to 4 as to whether the officer was legally right or wrong in his decision. The civilian police review board as mentioned prior is a group of lay people untrained in any of the aspects of law enforcement or the basic ideas of what our laws are about. These are the people who will judge as to whether a trained police officer acted properly or not. If it is obvious that the officer committed a moral or legal violation, the existing proper reviewing institutions will recognize it long before a board of untrained and non-police individuals will. If the officer was correct in his decision and acted properly in the course of his duties, the conclusion that a review board is unnecessary is even more obvious.

## THE CHALLENGE OF AUTHORITY

The real administrative authority within a police agency must come from the chief of police, or a comparable position. The man who has earned the title as the top administrator must be given the authority to command that position. When an officer commits a violation of policy or of moral wrong-doing, the agency must control his punishment. Without this control there is no reason for supervision and administrative positions. Naturally, if the offense is a criminal violation, the due processes of law should and will take place. Any contradiction of this system disturbs and violates the very nature of legal administrative powers and the concept of basic law.

## RESULTS OF ADOPTION

Police review boards usually create several undesirable changes within a police agency. The turnover rate of personnel accelerates rapidly with the departure of the more seasoned and educated officers. Recruitment of men with higher intelligence capacities becomes more difficult, and a strange atmosphere or attitude develops within the ranks of the remaining personnel.

When police officers believe that they can no longer obtain justice in the courts, or through the proper authorities, or that they will be subjected to unreasonable abuses by a civilian police review board, a new group morality begins to exist. Situations that may in any way be interpeted wrongly at a later date are avoided by the majority of the personnel. Of concern also is the decrease in essential productivity. When any activity may become subject to review by untrained individuals, the natural course of self-protection is to limit activity to only those which are mandatory. In the final evaluation of the effect of a civilian police review board it must be weighed against the question of how many excellent arrests are made through the *initiative* of a well-trained police officer.

*Chapter 8*

# THE POLICE AND POLITICS

$A$NY discussion or critical evaluation of the policeman's role in politics would be totally invalid and incomplete if it were not viewed from a historical perspective. Gerald O. Williams, author of the article "Political Police" in the March issue of *Police Magazine* states:

> Police from the earliest periods of history and organized government have existed as special bodies of officers, either civil or military, which have operated to detect and suppress political opposition to the government in power. Variously referred to a "Secret Police" and "Political Police" their objective has always been the same.

Political police have existed since the ancient Zoroastrian and Assyrian civilizations. According to Williams, the most complete information which we have today deals with the political police system as it existed in ancient Rome. Organized normally as a military addition, Tiberius Ceasar's political police intelligence arrangement had a widespread organization of agents engaged in the surveillance and supression of political and religious factors adverse to the Roman government.

The word "police" itself, which like "politics" is derived from the Greek noun *polis* or city-state gives us our first connotation of the involvement that political police might have played in the role of city-state governments throughout the Middle Ages and Renaissance. Although during these times it seems as though they were in many cases nothing more than assassins.

Governments of the eighteen and nineteenth centuries also utilized political police to counter the assaults of counter revolutions and revolts which were against the best interests of the established government. Williams continues in his article and says, "Political Police organizations can thus be shown to be much older in their origin than are the organizations for the enforcement of the criminal law with which we are so familiar today."

Political police, which were developed during the French and German empires of the eighteenth and nineteenth centuries were subsequent developments of assassins and criminals being utilized for removal of political opposition. These organizations have become very important and omnipotent today in countries like Russia and China and virtually have a stranglehold on the lives of their citizens. Quoting from Williams' article we find that

> When the political police of the Austro-Hungarian Empire, which served as a model for the security police systems of the 19th Century Prussia and Germany, was being organized by Emperor Joseph II in the 1780's, the first formal dichotomy of function as between the political and criminal police was established. At this time, the regular law enforcement organizations of Europe were being established, and a delineation of function between them and the older political police was called for.

In a memorandum on the establishment of the Austrian Higher State Police, this division was announced by Joseph II. A public police was to provide the protection which the subjects were due for their persons and property. On the other hand a secret or higher state police should protect the prince and his government from all dangers from subjects as well as from foreigners.

Modern-day Russian secret police and World War II German gestapo units were subsequent developments of Joseph II's political police system.

## AMERICAN HISTORY

According to a staff report to the President's Commission by James S. Campbell:

> Police participation in the political process in America has traditionally been limited and local. Limited to securing favorable legislation as to pension, working conditions and pay rates with occasional lobbying for or against proposals to abolish the death penalty, legalize gambling, or raise the age of juvenile court jurisdiction, and in the local sense, that it invariably involved approaches by the locally organized police to municipal authorities or at most to the state legislators representing the distict.

Many times charges would be made that the police were politically active in local campaigns, but generally the public has felt that the police should abstain from direct participation in politics. Early in the history of the United States, police were used against demonstrations, protests, strikes, and mobs, an example being the 1919 race riots. Many of these conflicts involved honest but misled groups of citizens. Many times instead of taking a neutral position in trying to restore domestic tranquility, during these primarily political clashes, the police have tended to become active participants on the side of management or on the side of the conservative elements against the dissident elements. Historically, the dissident elements have quickly recognized police siding with whom they consider the enemy, and consequently they have directed their assaults and abuse against the police. The cycle obviously becomes vicious with the police on the short end. This has been shown by the results of confrontation between management and labor disputes in the thirties and between California landowners and migrant farm workers in the early forties, as well as various other conflicts.

## Colonial Development

Political influence and law enforcement have seemed to be closely associated in the United States. During the early colonial period the sheriffs had a tremendous amount of political influence and frequently used their powers for political as well as personal gain. With the growth of the early towns the pronounced effect of their influences also grew. In those early days in America the sheriff, township constable, or village marshal, who were subject to popular election, were required to be engaged in politics.

## Development of the Sheriff in America

In America the office of sheriff, a political office, has only lived because it has been a rich prize for the political system that controlled it. Raymond Moley states in his *Book Politics and Criminal Prosecution:* "Ample political figures have found the office to their liking, including President Cleveland, who held the office of Sheriff or Erie County in (Buffalo)."
Largely because of the profits inherent in the fee system of

compensating county officers, the functions of process server and jailer have replaced that of a peace officer and his value as a peace officer has become negligible, according to Moley. A field survey, *Police and the Community*, done by the University of California at Berkeley states:

> The Sheriff is the chief law enforcement officer of the county and as such has technically concurrent jurisdiction with city police in incorporated areas. He is also responsible for taking and caring for prisoners in the county jail.

Volume II of this report states:

> In Philadelphia the sheriff is elected for a four year term and primarily is the execution arm of Philadelphia's courts. He serves court orders, warrants, writs and subpoenaes. He seizes real and personal property and sells it to obtain satisfaction on judgments, defaulted mortgages or unpaid taxes.

Constables are also elected and they serve as executive officers of the Magistrates Court. By common law, constables in many cities still have power of peace officers. According to Roger Lane in his book *Policing the City;* "In practice, during the early 19th Century, the appointment of Sheriff was for life."

## Early American Police Politicalization

As related in a staff report to the President's Commission on Crime, *The Politics of Protest:*

> Political involvement of the police is not per se a new phenomenon in the United States. Indeed, it is well known that in the days of the big city political machines Police were in politics in a small way. They often owed their jobs to local alderman and were expected to cooperate with political ward bosses.

Yet there was traditionally another way — perhaps an even more significant way in which police were political — as an active arm of the Status Quo."

One of the early records of police actively involved in politics, states Lane, was in the 1850's in Boston, when the local marshal and his men decided to "dabble in politics" by having his men vote a certain way in a popular election. This action was subsequently frowned upon by the mayor, and he fired the whole night force in retaliation. In the 1860's a theory was expressed that "the relation of the Chief of Police to the Mayor, but its very nature required the most implicit confidence, should not be disturbed by any doubt of his friendliness of feeling." Here we see some of the first philosophical ideas about the separation of police from the influence of politics. Lane continues: "In 1863 the majority of the people in Boston felt that criminals held the political balance and the police were used for political purposes."

In 1878 a police commission was established to facilitate reforms in the police department. Some of the improvements were getting new facilities, provision of firearms and the adoption of new promotion policies void of any political influence. The lessons learned in Boston were lessons already learned by other cities, and that lesson according to Lane was that "political change at the top was not enough to solve Police problems."

Charles Reith states in his book *The Blind Eye of History:*

> Metropolitan police forces, most of which developed during the late 1800's when government corruption was most prevalent, have often been deeply involved in political corruption. This corruption being manifested in Police political appointments given as a reward for political favors.

Patronage appointments seemed to lower the quality of personnel and tended to entice participation of police officers with politicians although this is still an accepted practice today in many small cities.

Many of the problems which troubled our first organized metropolitan police forces according to a Task Force Report, *The Police,* presented to the Crime Commission, can be traced to a single root – "political control." As Bruce Smith in his book, *Police Systems in the United States,* related:

> Rotation in office enjoyed so much popular favor that police posts of both high and low degree were constantly changing hands, with political fixers determining the price and conditions of exchange. The whole police question became identified with the corruption and degradation of the city politics and local governments of that period.

City leaders attempting to alleviate these problems sought to create police administrative boards to replace control exercised over police affairs by mayors or city councils. The President's

Commission on Law Enforcement and Administration of Justice states that "this attempt to cure political meddling was unsuccessful because the people who comprised the boards were inexpert in dealing with the board problems."

## Turn of the Century

On every side, the American administrative powers, at the turn of the nineteenth century was marked by lack of organization, decentralized responsibility, and inherent attitude on the part of public officials to cooperate. Roscoe Pound relates in his book, *Criminal Justice:* "Policemen as a rule changed as often as did the bosses of political power." Policemen who tried to fight the political system in this era, were in many cases transferred to punishment beats or other nondesirable positions.

According to Fred E. Haynes in his book, *Criminology,* police commissioners in New York up into the 1930's had an average term in office of about one year and seven months as compared to the police commissioner in London with an average of fifteen years on the same job.

## RECENT EVENTS

In the early fifties a theory was expressed by Adlai E. Stevenson, a noted Liberal politician, in his article "The Menace of Organized Crime" that "Crime and Politics must be divorced. Police forces on what ever level of government must be severed from partisian control." For example, prior to 1952 no major policy decision or personnel promotion was made in the police department of Philadelphia without the approval of the mayor and the political cronies out in the city's wards. This included promotion and assignment to district police captains. Volume II of the California field survey further states that the police department was politically dominated and controlled in the sixty-seven years prior to 1952.

In response to this onslaught against police politicalization many police organizations incorporated into existing regulations strict rules prohibiting political activity except voting. In the last decade, mostly as a result of efforts to raise police pay scales to an even level with skilled workmen, more militant police associations, according to Paul Chevigny, became "trade union affiliated," others in loose state and national affiliations escalated their pressure tactics so that job action "blue flu" (police call in sick in total) and even threatened police strikes became common place in police municipality salary disputes.

The major attempts for police politicalization, however, was without doubt the cause of civilian review boards. As stated by the *Washington Post:* "The proposals for civilian review boards were fought against in the legislature, courts and news media." Some proponents of the civilian review boards felt that a politicalized police force united, well financed and closely related to conservative social and political forces in the community, posed a problem for those interested in preserving democracy.

A new role was starting to be perceived by the "Thin Blue Line" into the fifties and sixties. That role was one of a minority group, and their feeling was constantly being reinforced by an apathetic, unaware, unconcerned public who were unaware of police problems. Police began to become reinforced into a defensive group with cohesive solidarity.

## THE POLICEMAN'S NEW ROLE

In a staff report, *Rights in Concord,* a response to the counter inaugural protest, the policeman's new role in dealing with a mass of demonstrators for example, is basically that of an umpire. Since the umpire must be the instant decision maker who stands in the eye of a potential storm, the policeman's job is an incredibly difficult one. To perform his task properly, a policeman should not become involved in the issues.

The conduct of government officials other than the police can make the policeman's job possible or impossible. Public officials can set the stage and lay down the rules for a demonstration in such a way that violent clashes between police and demonstrators are virtually certain to occur. Or public officials can condition responses of police and demonstrators in the direction of mutual toleration.

## PRESENT INVOLVEMENT

Having covered the historical role that police have played in the world of politics from the era of kings and emperors to recent times, it is only fitting that we now view the present-day policeman and the role he has or continues to play in politics. As a general statement or rule, the power of the politician over police in the country as a whole has greatly diminished. It was only during the 1940's that this reform in most major cities won the police their independence from the old-line political machines and bosses. However, as is often the case, there are exceptions to this rule.

As a starting point of present-day police involvement in politics it is felt worthwhile to quote James Q. Wilson, a Harvard political scientist, whose recently published book, *Varities of Police Behavior,* preceptively analyzes the police attitude. In it he detects a very definable "police attitude." He states "that the policeman develops from their work environment, whatever moral or emotional responses they may have brought to the job." The fact is that policemen in every city work within a social system which has already largely been defined by custom and practice before he entered it. This "police attitude" while informal in nature disposes the policeman toward rugged individualism, moral absolutism, and political conservatism. The conservatism is abstract and attached to distant ideals of honor and courage that rise above the reality of a society he feels is composed of uncooperative witnesses, of curious news media and reporters, and lastly of scheming politicians.

We could categorize the police in politics into two subheadings – *direct* and *indirect.* In distinguishing between the two we considered the following under *direct:*

1. Elected by citizens to a law enforcement position, example being the sheriff of a county.

2. Appointed to position in law enforcement by elected public official, example being the commissioner, public safety director, or chief of police appointed by the mayor or in the case of some cities a city manager or commission.

3. Those elected to other public office having previously served

as a law enforcement officer in some capacity, example being the present Mayor of Minneapolis, Minnesota, the Honorable Charles S. Stenvig.

Within the *indirect* role of police in politics were considered actions taken by individuals or groups of police to openly support a political candidate or party and in some cases even joining various types of organizations (social and fraternal), unions, or other organizations such as the John Birch Society and the Minutemen.

## Direct Involvement

1. Returning to the first heading under the direct involvement where we have a policeman *elected to a law enforcement position,* let us look briefly at the job cited — that of county sheriff. While he is an elected public official, he often is lacking in actual law enforcement experience or refuses to update himself in current aspects of it. He may often let the ideal of being reelected become paramount to his performance of duty as a police officer. This is not to say that elections corrupt a police officer who is an elected official but it does at least have a substantial influence on his life and job performance. Some county sheriffs have also given a "black eye" to law enforcement by their unscrupulous methods of retaining power and making financial gains to their individual benefit.

2. In the second subdivision we find those *appointed to positions in law enforcement by an elected public official* such as a mayor, city manager, or board of commissions. When this happens, it goes without saying that being political appointees they owe their allegiance and loyalty to the man or men who appointed them. This may at times have an adverse effect on their performance of duty, though by the same token it may place them in an effective position to apply political influence gained largely on their record in the position.

In this context we will look at several large cities in the United States and see how the police and politics are entwined and the impact each has on the other. The cities discussed will be Philadelphia, New York, Los Angeles, Chicago, and San Francisco.

A passing comment will be made concerning the recent survey of Omaha conducted by the International Association of Chiefs of Police. The police have the responsibility for the maintenance of order in the community. Differences of viewpoint and conflicts of interest make for a certain amount of controversy between the police and public.

The police may be called to protect the right to strike and picket in labor-management disputes. They may be confronted with the "marchers," sit-ins, and on election day it is they who add confidence and assure the peaceable use of the vote. However, as times have changed, the police have begun to take stands on more general social questions, sometimes in the political arena itself as we shall see in the discussion of the various cities.

**Philadelphia**: In 1967, Mayor James Tate won reelection over a reform ticket by compaigning heavily on the record of the popular police commissioner, Frank Rizzo. Although Rizzo took no personal role in the campaign, he is now regarded in the city as a political force to be reckoned with and is treated with careful deference by the Mayor.

Despite the new popularity, the police have been slow to turn to direct political action. Civil service regulations generally prohibit participation in party politics, and the police themselves are not anxious to return to the days when they were merely an arm of the local political organization. The Fraternal Order of Police, by far the nation's largest line organization has zeroed in on the Philadephia Police Advisory Board as bad and symbolic of the review board menace facing the police.

**Los Angeles**: The party machines have never been a powerful force, but the police along with other groups of city employees have formed voter blocs that have often been important in the determining of the outcome of local elections. By and far however, they have concentrated on gaining higher wages and other material benefits in return for this support. As governmental employees they, as all other police in major cities, have usually tried to stay on the right side of city hall. Perhaps an example of involvement by a personage no less than the late police chief William Parker would be in order. He participated actively in the Christian Anti-Communist Crusade in 1960 and encouraged his police officers to attend their schools at special reduced police "fees." He, like many other noted police authorities and concerned Americans, considered the American Civil Liberties Union as a Communist front organization and was in favor of maintaining the "status quo" in regards to the ethnic groups.

**New York:** There are those who feel that even the most professional police department cannot be trusted to perform in the public interest if elected officials do not have a firm control of law enforcement policy. The police, like the military, should not be permitted to determine their own policies in a democratic society. Unfortunately, this control of policy by elected officials is confused in the minds of many policemen and many ordinary citizens because of the kind of political domination of police departments reminiscent of the early 1930's. For such a case in point we look at the city of New York.

Leftist Activist Mayor John Lindsay sought to assert his authority over his police department when in 1966 he installed his own police commissioner and made other changes in the department.

His results have been spotty at best against organized police opposition. The Patrolman's Benevolent Association did exert enough pressure however, to have the civilian board he established to review a complaint against the police abolished by a voter referendum.

**San Francisco:** The police had been controlled previous to 1956 by a three-man commission appointed by the mayor. Usually it consisted of one member who was above reproach and two political appointees by the mayor. Thus it can be readily observed that the mayor controlled the police and used them for his own ends. However, in 1956, a new reform mayor appointed three impeccable citizens to fill the commission slots. They in turn appointed a reform chief of police, Ahern, who kept the post until his death in 1958 when Thomas Cahill was appointed to replace him.

Police influence has been profound in many areas though it was usually in an indirect method scheme of things. In conjunction with these closer community efforts they formed special squads to work the minority groups as well as convicts just released from prison. They provided understanding of each others problems and helped to rehabilitate the ex-con with job opportunities he might not otherwise have received.

Various of the reform measures sought by the police have received only lukewarm reception by Chief Cahill and the community relations squads were returned to the control of the district captains under conserted pressures by them.

In showing their independence the police displayed Ronald Regan for Governor stickers on the police vehicles in the 1966 election and ceased only reluctantly when Cahill issued a department directive forbidding it.

**Chicago**: Prior to 1960 the Chicago police were the epitome of police corruption and were generally held in contempt by the community. Traditional alliances between the police and politicians made the chief little more than a figurehead. Officers who had political influence knew they had little to worry about as long as their political counterpart remained in power. However, the downfall and reform of the police department happened in late 1959 when a number of policemen were found to be members of a large burglary operation.

Reforms followed, based on a commission set up by Mayor Daley. He appointed Orlando Wilson as chief of police who in turn started setting about making reforms despite opposition of the Patrolman's Benevolent Association.

Some reforms took place, it is true, but there are those who have expressed the belief that the mayor calls the shots right over the chief's head. This may have caused Chief Wilson to resign in 1967, and the feeling presented can be borne out by the handling of the demonstrations at the 1968 Democratic convention.

The influence of the mayor and other elected public officials varies, but the important thing is that today it's seemingly aboveboard, whereas in the past it tended to be of personal nature and was secretive as a rule. The objection of political control and domination of the police does not include, however, that the police function can or should be entirely divorced from the political process.

3. We shall now look at the last section of *direct* involvement — those *elected to other public office after having previously served*

*in a law enforcement position.* For this we will look at the city of Minneapolis, Minnesota.

Mayor Charles S. Stenvig was a forty-one-year-old former burglary detective who ran on a third party reform platform with a campaign based on the "law and order" issue and backed by an army of volunteers on the street. His popularity after five months in office has not waned since he got 62 percent of the vote in the election. This is based on a full-scale revision of police procedure and support the police are getting from the mayor and other department higher-ups.

This tends to show in one case that the policeman from the office can be successful in the public elected office of mayor.

Now for a word about the survey of the Omaha Police Department conducted by the IACP. Once of the most pronounced recommendations was that some of the top civil service positions be removed from that status and placed there by mayoral appointment. It was sighted that this was not to get police back in politics but to allow for easier recruitment from college campus personnel with administrative training. The mayor in a later news conference indicated that he and the chief of police were not in favor of it as they felt it would put politics back in the police force. Though no decision has been affirmed, it is apparent that all positions save the Chief and Director of Public Safety will probably remain under the civil service merit promotion system.

### Indirect Involvement

Let us now look at the *indirect* methods of police involvement in the politics of our society. While it is true that a minority of policemen are actual members of organizations such as the John Birch Society, some discussion is felt in order. The John Birch Society holds ideals for the policemen by virtue of its sympathetic propaganda. One such publication of the Society decreed in California in 1965 that "demands for police review boards, false allegations of police brutality, rash Supreme Court decisions, demand for recall of police administrators and numerous other acts of harassment have made the police officer's job tremendously more difficult in these times of lawlesness in the streets." It is this type of literature which has great appeal for the hard-pressed policeman of our society. The same is true of the various other law and order oriented organizations.

The various fraternal organizations have also given the policeman a voice in the field of politics; as an example the case mentioned concerning the New York PBA which received enough popular support to defeat the review board in a voters referendum. The Fraternal Order of Police is doing likewise in the city of Philadelphia.

## Procedures

The question facing the police officer is not one of whether or not to become involved in politics, but rather whether to be actively involved or passively involved. Police officers who chose to become actively involved include the mayor of Detroit, the mayor of Minneapolis, and a city councilman in Los Angeles, among others. The choice for them was not only one of active versus passive political involvement, however, for active partisan political activity is prohibited by regulation or policy in almost every major police department. Their choice caused them to leave law enforcement to enter the political arena. Let us assume that a police officer does desire to engage in political activity and does not wish to leave his profession. Can he do it? The answer is yes. There are restrictions and pitfalls, but the police officer can make his voice heard and his opinion felt without coming into open conflict with the municipality or state that employs him. The police officer can act as an individual or as a group member. He can participate in nonpartisan political activity, or in partisan political activity. The avenues to political activity are many and varied.

The first step to consider is the right to vote. The vote of the individual is sometimes downgraded or ignored as a vital item in the political picture. The importance of the vote of the individual, however, cannot be downgraded or ignored. It is vital!

From elections which decide the presidency of the United States to elections which determine the next city councilman, the vote of only a comparative few can be decisive. In the winner-take-all concept of our system of electing presidents by electoral vote, the popular plurality which sways the electoral vote is particularly interesting. During the 1968 elections, the pivotal state of Illinois threw its 26 votes to Nixon. The results could have been reversed, however, by only a change of one vote in each precinct. The 1948 upset of Thomas E. Dewey by Harry Truman was a close one also. Dewey lost Ohio by 7,107 votes and California by 17,865 votes, a margin of approximately one vote per precinct. The individual vote is even more important in the election of legislators. Those gentlemen, who have an even more direct effect of the legislation of concern to policemen, are often elected by an even closer margin. In 1956, Representative Hale of Maine was reelected by 29 votes; Congressman Sieminski of New Jersey won by 57 votes; and Representative Doliver of Iowa lost by 198 votes.

A selective effort to get out the vote can be very effective. During the 1968 presidential elections only 61 percent of the electorate voted. During the off-year of 1966 only 46 percent of eligible voters voted. The vote in state primaries seldom runs more than 30 percent, and is often lower in local elections. It is obvious that selective voter registration drives and pressure to get out the voters of each party can be the most rewarding effort.

A personal communication to the elected legislator can be instrumental in the passage or failure of proposed legislation. Recently, in the state of Nebraska, a group of less than 100 citizens was successful in forcing reconsideration of a bill that had already been voted down in the state legislature. Fewer than 100 letters and telegrams caused a bill to be passed that will influence one and one-half million Nebraskans! A letter or telegram from even one voter can be influential. To help insure that it gets the attention that it warrants, there are several dos and don'ts that should be heeded. A legislator will normally place more weight on correspondence bearing upon pending legislation than upon general topics. Pending legislation should be identified by either its popular name or its number. If the bill is not properly identified, there is a possibility that a representative will not be able to identify it either. Comments should be concise and logical. A personal letter or telegram should be just that — personal. Form letters and coupons from papers and magazines, urging a particular view, are handy for head counts, but do not carry the same weight a personal communication does. Lastly, a communication should not be abusive.

Petitions and referendums offer a comparatively speedy way of forcing action on a subject when it has wide public support. The circulation of petitions by police officers would, in most instances, be prohibited or discouraged. A police officer's signature and support as a private citizen does help, however. Recently, in New York City, the mayor installed a police review board which was heavily weighted with anti-police and minority members. In the face of heavy opposition the mayor stated that his action was not subject to review by the voters. Subsequent legal action, a petition, and a referendum vote proved him wrong. Voters of both major political parties, the Conservative Party, and the John Birch Society rallied behind the Police Benevolent Association and threw out the civilian review board by a vote of better than two to one.

Individual, nonpartisan political activity can be effective. The same amount of effort exerted in concert with others, however, can be even more effective. Normally, joining with others in combined political activity will involve political party affiliation. Selection of a political party involves several considerations. Most important among these considerations is the compatability of the party philosophy with your own and the effectiveness of the party in promoting its program.

Historically, our country has always had two major parties, and occasionally, a third minor party which represents a radical or reactionary element which cannot be readily accomodated by one of the major parties. Senator Hugh D. Scott, the present Senate Minority Leader and a renowned political writer, has stated: "Independent movements usually fail through lack of continuity, grass-roots organization, and political know-how." The Socialist Party, the Dixiecrats of 1948, and Henry Wallace's Progressive Party of 1948 are cases in point. The two major parties have a great absorbant capacity. A persistent third party will find that, over a period of time, it has lost its platform. The planks have been incorporated in the platform of the major parties. Norman

Thomas, the perennial presidential candidate of the Socialist Party, stated shortly before his death that he did not feel it was necessary for him to run in the election, for one or both of the major parties had adopted his entire earlier platform.

On the state and local level, third party membership may be more successful. Even here, however, they are seldom able to muster a majority and are most effective in instances where they are able to force one of the major parties to bend to their position. This is normally done by being able to present a bloc of voters to one side or the other, rather than through fear that their candidate will win.

Normally, the next step after joining a political party would be to participate in supporting party activities, probably at the precinct level. It is at this point, however, that we run head-on into the general ban on active, partisan political activity by police officers. It is necessary then to consider another form of political activity that does not expose the police officer to charges of active, partisan political activity, but at the same time is the most practical and effective form of political pressure, namely participation in a pressure group that maintains an active lobby.

## Lobbies in American Government and Politics

When divisions within a society become so conscious of their desires that they perfect a definite organization, draw up a platform of objectives and actively seek to bring about the realization of their aspirations by influencing elected and appointed officials, they have attained the status of a pressure group.

Stated above is one definition of what a pressure group is. Generally a pressure group is conceived of as a specific group of persons who feel that their particular concern about public policy is the best. This group then goes about attempting by various methods to attain their goal. This organization may be well organized or loosely organized. The group may represent a large economic concern or be practically penniless. Regardless of these factors it must merely be a group of interested persons who share basic attitudes and convictions on a common topic. Generally the pressure group is short lived and rather temporary. This is caused mainly by the fact that the group is made up of persons who have become aroused over a single issue. When that issue is resolved, they disseminate until such time as they may organize again, with other individuals, to promote a different issue. Other pressure groups are more lasting such as the American Medical Association. This group has a large, well-organized following, adequate financial support, and prestige. Groups such as this do not tend to break up, but remain consolidated and pursue new issues when other issues are disposed of.

Law enforcement in general might be called a pressure group. The members of law enforcement organizations tend to have the same feelings about a number of issues. However, they also, to date, fall under the heading of the type of pressure group which is not well organized. From time to time an issue arises that solidifies persons involved in law enforcement, but on the whole, there is not a strong enough national organization. This may be remedied with the advent of a national police organization. Members of the rank and file in law enforcement need this type of organization to look after their interests before state and national legislatures. A well-organized group would also help in the establishment of better public opinion in favor of law enforcement.

Related to pressure groups are lobbies. Lobbies are similar to pressure groups in that they attempt to sway public opinion and influence public policy. However, the comparison stops there. Where the pressure group is generally short lived, the lobby tends to be sustaining. Where the pressure group generally is limited to one topic, the lobby is interested in the many facets of an issue. As an example, a pressure group of aroused citizens may attempt to influence a legislature to lower the speed limit near a playground, when this is accomplished they disband. But a lobby of the American Medical Association might attempt to influence a legislature for stricter drug control, and at the same time be interested in and lobbying for five or six other bills before the legislature. One should remember that "not all pressure groups are lobbies, but all lobbies are pressure groups."

Pressure groups form a lobby in Washington or state legislatures and are represented generally by lawyers, who prefer to call themselves legislative counsel rather than lobbyist. This is caused mainly by the fact that at one time, and with many people today, lobbyists had a bad reputation. People tend to think of lobbyists as unscrupulous and exerting undue influence of legislators. They believe that the purpose of a lobby is to bribe and force a legislator by any means to adopt the policy of the lobby. This has been true in the past and occasionally may be true today, but for the most part, this means of lobbying has been replaced with more acceptable means.

For the the lobbyists' own good most of the state legislatures and the national congress have passed laws which regulate lobbying. This is accomplished through legislation which forces the individual lobbyist to register and keep on file a record of expenditures which are connected to his lobbying. Penalty for omitting to register or file financial reports has been made a criminal offense in some states, and is punishable, generally by up to one year imprisonment and/or a fine.

The National Police Officers Association has a lobby in Washington and is basically the only formal police lobby in Washington. Other police pressure groups such as the IACP could and should have a lobby in Washington. National organizations should concentrate on the national congress and administration. However, local police pressure groups, such as local department associations (PBA's and benevolent leagues) could pressure and lobby in their own states and communities. This should be done, because the local departments know best where to and how to apply pressure in their own geographic area.

The pressure group and lobbyist can be an asset to the legislature and legislator. He generally has a wealth of information on the issue which he is representing. He has much more insight into the problems of the group he is representing and is better able to get the group's point across than is the group itself.

The police and law enforcement officials and the society as a whole would benefit from a law enforcement lobby in Washington. This lobby would have to be a full-time job and suited to the purpose of arguing for and pleading the cause of law enforcement. This lobby could have the effect of influencing and obtaining legislation which would be favorable to law enforcement, rather than some of the anti-police legislation that has been coming forth. This lobby could also appear before the courts as a friend of the court and explain the police position.

With the strength of the National Police Officers Association and other professional police organizations a strong lobby and more effective pressure group will probably come forth. As a law enforcement lobby, the lobby will probably be scrutinized more closely than the average lobby for unsavory practices and corruption.

Lobbying is very much like a public relations and advertising job. The techniques used by public relations men, advertisers, and lobbyists are very similar. All are aimed at winning favorable public opinion. All attempt to become and should be very adept at becoming, experts in the art of influence. A successful lobbyist knows how to write up a favorable bill and to whom to take it to get it started on its way to becoming law. The lobbyist must know from whom to seek help on different facets of legislation concerning law enforcement.

The lobbyists must also learn how to institute effectively the various techniques of influence. A few of these techniques are listed below with some brief explanations:

1. Attempting to influence individual legislators.
2. Testifying before committees.
3. Public advertising — television, radio, movies, pamphlets, articles, news.
4. Pressuring of constituents:
   a. Rifle — letters from chosen influential constituents to the legislator.
   b. Shotgun — appeal to all constituents to write to their congressman in an attempt to overwhelm the legislators.
5. Attempting to influence individual administrators.
6. Using courts to test constitutionality of a law.

These are but a few of the methods which might be implemented.

## ADVANTAGES OF POLITICAL INVOLVEMENT

No longer can police take a defensive stand on every issue thrown at them. The time for debating on whether police should be outspoken or not is past history. Any group which had made strides in advancement has done so in an outright effort.

Unfortunately the word "politics" puts fear into the average lawman's heart and thoughts of graft into the citizen's mind. In its simplest definition politics means conducting the business of a government. Certainly the business of that government has to be enforced. Logically then, police are already involved in the mainstream of politics. The question then changes from how should we get into politics to how do we get involved?

There is only one path to follow. That is to come out in the open and stand up for those issues which are of police concern. Many candidates ran in the fall of 1969 on law and order tickets. A few policemen resigned their positions and were elected to office. Police are going to become more and more involved in this area. The people obviously are prepared to accept active involvement on the part of police in politics.

Certainly partisan politics will have to be eliminated, except in that police will be partisan for police concerns. No double standard can exist in the criminal justice system. Many people will undoubtedly be shocked at vocal involvement. These will be the anti-police minority though, and not the great silent majority.

One benefit of hearing a policeman speak out on issues is enlightenment. Many people in the "silent majority" are really ignorant of the many facets making up police work. They have never been confronted with law enforcement directly and simply have not had to think about it. These people have all heard the worn-out statements about how underpaid and worthy our police are, but it was normally only small talk and went in one ear and out the other.

During the last decade it has become fashionable to voice grievances in a boisterous way. The larger the group and the more aggressive their demands the greater their benefits seem to be. Police should not use coercion to achieve goals. But a few hints done in a well thought out manner can not help but assist police goals. This is the "now generation" for everyone else, so why not policemen. There is some truth in the old cliche "the squeaky wheel gets the grease."

A hard decision to make of course is where do we draw a line between what is political activity and what is dereliction of the sworn police duty. This line will probably not be clear until such time as the court system has decided them. During the meantime there will need to be ground rules formulated for activation. We will take a logical approach to separation. Any activity which would without question be detrimental to public safety has to be ruled out. At the other extreme, activities which have little or no effect on public safety should be utilized. A good example of this might be to refuse a motorcycle escort for a dignitary who is a known anti-police supporter. This would drive across the point to him and his supporters that police have ways of communicating their feelings also.

A cohesive organization can muster support in numerous ways. They can send lobbyists to sway legislation. They have centrally directed goals and usually a solvent treasury to finance their means.

Many people who are afraid of police having any political power are hurting themselves. Suppose that a city has a high crime rate and very few policemen. The police they do have are local men hired at minimum wages. Consequently, they do as little enforcement work as necessary and it is of poor quality. It seems logical that the low wages have a direct bearing on the number and type of personnel employed by this city. Now, lobbyists push for a state standard and a bill authorizing an equal number of police per population. The city has to take a little tax bite, but now they hire outstanding applicants at a decent wage and get some qualified .personnel. The crime rate is reduced, the city gets its money back in the long run, and the citizens are safer.

The police are much larger in numbers than many groups, but they are not united in a concentrated effort. At present there is no well-recognized national spokesman for police, but he or they will emerge as police become actively involved in seeking their goals.

The catalysts for police to stand up and be counted is everywhere. The anti-police elements in addition to recent court decisions have made police realize that they are no longer able to sit back and just bear the brunt of a changing society. Quite possibly the recent Supreme Court decisions are a blessing in disguise. The new breed of police are being trained to deal in a technical society where any breach of due process can free a criminal. Also this new breed is demanding compensation for its preparation efforts. Police salaries are being raised everywhere.

With an ever-expanding population our crime problem is multiplying. Even though the quality of police is improving the fact remains that crime does pay. It is estimated that a good organization can apprehend and bring prosecution in less than one third of all felony cases. This concern for growing crime has made law enforcement a bigger concern for the citizen.

Unless police choose to become actively involved in our increasingly complex society and its changing attitudes, they may receive less sympathy and understanding than they did in the past. Police have got to share their knowledge and experience with legislatures and courts. The police community is not a group apart from society, it is part of it. The time to act is now.

# Chapter 9

# ORGANIZED CRIME

AMERICA has given birth and refuge to many different groups, cults, beliefs, and organizations in the two hundred years of its existence. None of these has presented such a threat to our way of life as the development of an organization which, since it was first recognized in 1890, has become bigger, richer, and more sinister until today it is so powerful that it touches almost everyone and affects the whole of American life. Many Americans still find it difficult to believe that their nation harbors an evil entity capable of stealing billions while destroying the honor of public officials, the honesty of businessmen, and sometimes the lives of ordinary citizens. Yet the evidence has become all too credible (5).

It exists for the sole purpose of robbing the American citizen of everything he holds and if needed, of even his life. It recognizes none of the moral or ethical codes of any society other than its own; practically every type of business and industry in the United States is currently being exploited or penetrated by an awesome, powerful, and no-holds-barred competitor — a conglomerate of crime. This criminal conglomerate employs thousands, nets billions annually, operates nationally and internationally, possesses an efficient and disciplined organizational structure, wields a depressingly effective lobbying apparatus, insulates itself against legal action, destroys billion-dollar corporations and cripples smaller companies and, according to many, rates as the most serious long-term danger to the security and principles of this nation (6).

The vast majority of the American people would say that we are now living in a period encompassed by acts of violence and civil

---

5. "Cosa Nostra – The Poison in Our Society," *Reader's Digest* (December, 1969), p. 119.
6. *Deskbook on Organized Crime* (Washington, D.C.: Chamber of Commerce of the United States, 1969), p. 3.

disorders. Our present total disregard for law and order was surpassed only during the era of prohibition when this society was plagued with such notorious gangsters as Al Capone, John Dillinger, "Maw" Barker, and hoodlum gangs that spread terror and lawlessness throughout this nation. But it was during this era that the real and most dangerous threat to every community within the United States was born. It is difficult to believe that the imperfections of our social institutions and of our government have provided the basis for the origin and development of an organization which has become known as the "second government" (7). Its management has been the least understood and recognized of any malady within our society. Echoed warnings by many authorities investigating this criminal threat have been made public, but to no avail. A former chairman of the highly respected and effective New York State Commission of Investigation issued this sobering statement: "With the exception of the war in Vietnam, crime in the streets and organized crime are probably the most serious problems which confront the country today . . . in the long run, organized crime is probably the most serious, and unquestionably one of the most dangerous" (8).

What is organized crime? How did it develop? Why has it become so capable of such moral and economic destruction that it demands total submission to its desires and controls? This chapter intends to illustrate the areas covered by the above questions and to show how this group has obtained its stranglehold on America, its origin, its present location, its legitimate and illegitimate businesses, the way it daily affects the lives of every American, what can be done to overcome this organization, and a recommended course of action that must be taken if this society is to survive as a free and democratic form of government.

Over the centuries renowned authorities have continually issued warnings to our political leaders and the American public that there is a force within our country known as the Mafia, the Mob, the Syndicate, the Outfit, the Confederation, the Black Hand, an

---

7. In 1963 Joseph Valachi publicly revealed the inner workings of what he called "This second government," known to its members as La Cosa Nostra. It is also referred to in Ed Reid's book *The Grim Reapers* (1969), p. 22.

8. *Deskbook on Organized Crime,* p. 4.

Organization, a Criminal Cartel, a Conspiracy, a Cult, a Brotherhood, and today these organizations have become best known as La Cosa Nostra or simply – "Organized

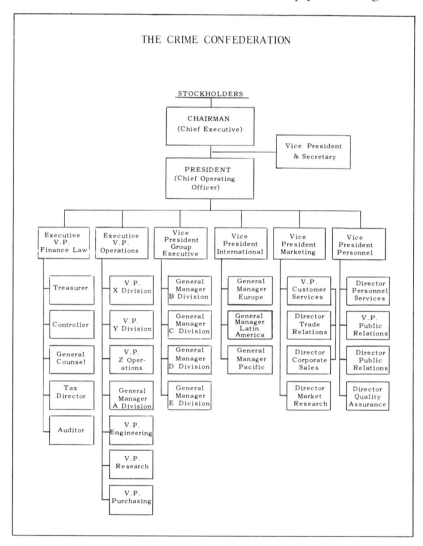

Figure 3. The organizational structure of a legitimate business and the division of responsibility, delegation of authority, and coordination of activities within a company. (From Salerno and Tompkins: *Crime Confederation*. Doubleday, New York, 1969, p. 84.)

Crime" (9). In May, 1965, a term was defined by a group of forty of the nation's most renowned law enforcement authorities:

> The product of a self perpetuating criminal conspiracy to wring exorbitant profits from our society by any means — fair and foul, legal and illegal. Despite personnel changes, the conspiratorial entity continues. It is a malignant parasite which fattens on human weakness. It survives on fear and corruption. By one or another means, it obtains a high degree of immunity from the law. It is totalitarian in its organization. A way of life, it imposes rigid discipline on underlings who do the dirty work while the top men of organized crime are generally insulated from the criminal act and the consequent danger of prosecution (10).

The existence of this organization was suspected as long ago as 1890, when a New Orleans Grand Jury concluded that an organization called "Mafia" existed. This acknowledgement came about from an investigation into the brutal slaying of a New Orleans Police Chief, Peter Hennessey, who was investigating two murders that occurred over contracts for the handling of cargo on the New Orleans docks. The Grand Jury stated:

> The range of our research has developed the existence of the secret organization styled "Mafia." The evidence comes from several sources fully competent in themselves to attest the truth, while the fact is supported by the long record of blood-curdling crimes, it being almost impossible to discover the perpetrators or to secure witnesses (11).

In 1915, a Chicago Crime Commission concluded that there was a loosely organized, interstate band of professional criminals. The Bureau of Narcotics and Dangerous Drugs considers the 1957 Apalachin Mafia meeting as but one of several dating back to 1928 (12). It was, however, a break-through for law enforcement in its

---

9. Research has provided the following names as being applied to organized crime: Peter Mass "The Story Behind the Crime Hearings," *Saturday Evening Post* (November 23, 1963), pp. 21-23; Sandy Smith, The Crime Cartel," *Life* (September 1, 1967), pp. 15-24; Peter Mass, *The Valachi Papers* (New York: Bantam Books, 1969), p. 1.

10. Ralph Salerno and John Tompkins, *The Crime Confederation* (New York: Doubleday, 1969), p. 313.

11. Ed Reid, *The Grim Reapers* (Chicago: Henry Regency Co., 1969), p. 8.

12. Organized crime as it is known today began to develop on December 5, 1928 when 23 top Mafia leaders met in Cleveland, Ohio. Their next meeting took place in 1931 at Atlantic City, New Jersey. It was here that organized crime set its policies and plans into a finalized form, while the FBI and other agencies were making public statements that the Syndicate had been defeated by the defeat of Capone. The next meeting took place

struggle to make politicians realize that there was such a thing as a "Criminal Cartel" within this country; it was this meeting and numerous other reports by both private and governmental investigations that bolstered the evidence pointing toward the existence of an organized underworld beyond crescendo proportions – evidence now ignored by only the naive, the uninformed, or by those paid to look the other way (13). President Nixon has in fact observed:

> Today, organized crime has deeply penetrated broad segments of American life. In our great cities, it is operating prosperous criminal cartels. In our suburban areas and smaller cities, it is expanding its corrosive influence. . . . It quietly continues to infiltrate and corrupt organized labor. It is increasing its enormous holdings and influence in the world of legitimate business (14).

It has been further concluded by other authoritative sources that

> Organized crime is a society that seeks to operate outside the controls of the American people and their governments. It involves thousands of criminals, working within structures as complex as those of any large corporation, subject to laws more rigidly enforced than those of legitimate governments. Its actions are not impulsive but rather the result of intricate conspiracies, carried on over whole fields of activity in order to amass huge profits. The core of organized crime activity is the supplying of illegal goods and services . . . but organized crime is also extensively and deeply involved in legitimate business and in labor unions . . . (15).

But the real and most dangerous threat of organized crime is not just the dealing in illicit goods and services. The danger arises

13. Reports stating that there was an organized criminal cartel dates back to the twelve separate reports filed by the Wickensham Commission during 1929-1931; Chicago Crime Commission Report, 1942; Kefauver's Commission reports, 1950-1951; and the present McClellan Commission report. Prior to the reports of the McClellan Commission and the forceful tactics by the late Robert F. Kennedy, then Attorney General of the United States, organized crime was considered to be a local problem and not nationally oriented.
14. *Deskbook on Organized Crime*, p. 3.
15. *Ibid.*, pp. 3-4.

in 1957 at Apalachin, New York, where more than 50 top leaders of the Mafia had gathered to divide up the territory of the late Albert Anastasia but were surprised by the arrest from Law Enforcement officers. The last known public gathering of Mafia members was held in a Queens New York restaurant in 1966. It is believed that this meeting was called to settle unfinished business from the 1957 Apalachin meeting.

because of the vast profits acquired from the sale of illicit goods and services which are being invested in legitimate enterprise, both in the business sphere and the governmental sphere. "It is when criminal syndicates start to undermine basic economic and political traditions and institutions, real trouble begins, and the real trouble has begun in the United States" (16).

The past history of the Mafia is clouded with mythology and legend (17). Some theorists hypothesize that its birth began as an underground resistance movement against one of the invaders that oppressed Sicily in the ninth century. It was a time when all of the inhabitants of this sun-drenched island were trodden under the despotic dictatorship of a cruel and harsh ruler from France (18). We are told that the Mafia during this period created an image of Robin Hood; it would take from the rulers by bribery, threats, arson, murder, and extortion, then divide its ill-gotten gains among the poor and subservient peasants. After many decades of this rule, the French were finally thrust from Italy and Sicily. Peace reigned throughout the land; now the Mafiosi found that they would have to return to honest toil, a task for which they were neither willing nor prepared to accept. The Mafia had found its way of life so profitable that it adopted the same methods and techniques which were fostered by its captors. Its victims, now instead of despotic rulers, were the shopkeepers, the farmers, and townspeople of the small villages and islands that it had previously protected and supported. Everyone was forced to pay tribute to the Mafia or suffer the consequences of total destruction of their property or their very lives.

It was not until the end of the nineteenth century and the

---

16. *Ibid.*, p. 4.

17. As Salerno and Tompkins indicate in the footnote on page 108 of their text, "The beginnings of the Mafia itself are lost in antiquity, though it probably started as an underground resistance movement against one of the invaders — Romans, Arabs, Norman, Spaniards, Neapolitan Bourbons, and Northern Italians — that have oppressed Sicily since the ninth century. The origin of the word Mafia is similarly vague. It has been identified as a Piedmontese word for gang, an Italian neologism for bravado, and a word coined in the thirteenth century from the initial letters of the phrase 'Morte alla Francia Italia anela' (Death to France Italy cries). The most likely explanation is that mafia means 'place of refuge' in Arabic, a reference to dispossessed farmers who fled to the hills rather than become serfs."

18. *Ibid.*, p. 109.

beginning of the twentieth century that the influence of the Mafia began to take hold within the boundaries of the United States. This was brought about by two major factors that occurred during this period. First was the immigration of Italians into the United States who were escaping the fascist methods employed by Benito Mussolini, dictator in Italy (19). Under the direction of Mussolini, a complete purge was instigated in Italy and Sicily to rid the country of the Mafia influence and domination. By use of fascist methods – arrest without warrant, confessions extracted by torture, imprisonment without trial – many of the Mafia members were jailed, and by the late 1920's the government had reduced the open activities of the organization to its lowest level. However, many shrewd Mafiosi saw what was in the future and joined the fascist movement so they could infiltrate the government itself. Even those who went to jail were able to survive the trials and tribulations encountered during this period. Through the aid of those Mafiosi who had obtained government positions, the convicted were usually able to continue controlling their gangs from within the prison. Most important, though, were those nimble and enterprising Mafia members who escaped by immigrating to the United States, mostly as illegal aliens. In 1925, the United States worsened this problem, by curtailing the immigration of Italians into this country by placing a restrictive quota upon their admittance. This contributed to the illegal entry of Mafiosi into the country (much as did Italian laws that placed a person suspected of involvement with the Mafia on a blacklist and would not allow them out of Italy (20).) Prior to this time, Italian immigrants who came to the country were different from other American ethnic groups – they tended to settle into areas where they could set up their own communal groupings. This cultured an ideal social structure for the rise of the Mafia terrorist movement in America.

In Sicily the Mafia is a tight-knit collection of gangsters preying on the peasants. So great is the power of the Mafia that when they commit a murder against one of their people it is accepted with no more than a shrug of the shoulder, a few tears, and the sign of the

19. *Ibid.,* p. 276.
20. *Ibid.,* pp. 276-77.

cross (21). There is also a tradition in Sicily, centuries old, that when a young man wishes to marry a girl who is unwilling to become his wife, he must abduct her, carry her off to the hills, and rape her. Then the crude and primitive justice of the Mafia takes over. The girl must marry her abductor to protect her honor. To refuse would endanger the life and property of her family and, furthermore, no other Sicilian would dare marry her (22). On one occasion where a girl was taken by a Mafioso member against her wishes, she decided not to follow the Sicilian tradition. As an inducement to make her change her mind, her father's farm equipment was mysteriously destroyed. His vegetable plants were uprooted. Animals were let loose to trample and eat his oat fields at night. Five hundred of his grapevines were mysteriously slashed at their bases. "I didn't dare complain," the father said. "They would have destroyed our house if I had" (23). Thus one can fully realize the ease with which the Mafia continues its hold upon Italian peasant immigrants inside the United States.

Second, a major factor that added to the influence and power of the Mafia in America was the passage of the Volstead Enforcement Act or Prohibition. This act prohibited the manufacturing, distribution, and use of any form of distilled spirits. These two ingredients came together in the "roaring twenties" — prohibition and a group of men already well schooled in organized criminal activities. The Mafia observed that prohibition laws were not being enforced, and that the majority of the people did not want them enforced. The results were natural. The illegal alcohol business was organized and run with the zest and bravado of men who suddenly found themselves living in a country where respect for individual liberty worked in their favor (24).

Parenthetically, the long-standing affinity of Jewish gangsters for Italian and Sicilian gangsters was cemented during this period. The Jews had also fled from oppressive European governments. The two groups had a common bond that went beyond their

21. "A Mother's Pain," *Newsweek* (May 2, 1960), p. 41.
22. "Justice for Francia," *Newsweek* (January 2, 1967), p. 37.
23. *Ibid.*
24. Salerno and Tompkins, pp. 277-279.

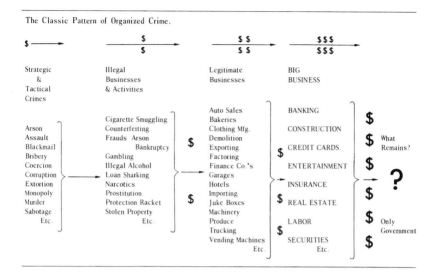

Figure 4. The flow of money from the criminal activites of organized crime into legitimate business sphere. Once the money has entered this field, the rake-off and skimming process of the organized crime cartel is channeled into either unidentified financial institutions inside of the United States or to foreign financial institutions. (From Salerno and Tompkins: *Crime Confederation.* Doubleday, New York, 1969, pp. 230-231.)

mutual interest in the profitability of prohibition. However, prohibition helped to foster organized crime by combining major criminal factions – Italians, Jews, Welsh, Irish, and other separate groups into a central controlled organization (25). Prohibition also provided the organization with its first real source of big money. Until this time, prostitution, gambling, extortion, and other criminal activities had not generated much capital even on their largest scale (26). With illegal liquor being a multi million dollar industry, it furnished the capital needed to expand its operations into other illegal activities, but primarily to penetrate legitimate businesses as a front for its continued operations. It also opened the way for corruption of politicians and police on a large scale. It began the Syndicate connections with politics and demoralized many law enforcement groups to a point from which they never

25. *Ibid.*
26. *Ibid.*

fully recovered (27).

Mass evasion of the Volstead Act put the average citizen in touch with criminals, resulting in tolerance and eventually admiration, even to the point of romantic approval of the mobsters. It permanently undermined the respect for law and order and the people charged with enforcing it. Ever since prohibition the man in the street has accepted the idea that policemen can be bought.

The manufacture and distribution of illegal liquor in the United States and the illegal entry of foreign-made liquor gave the men who were organizing crime experience in the administration and control of multi billion dollar, worldwide business, with thousands of employees and long payrolls. Men who had never before managed anything bigger than a family farm or a local gang got on-the-job training that turned them into leaders with developed executive qualities (28).

With the repeal of the Volstead Act and the death or arrest of the notorious gangsters that plagued the nation during the "roaring twenties," the public and most law enforcement men rejoiced that the Syndicate had finally been smashed. But little did they realize that this was not the end of the organization so destined to become the greatest cancer of our society.

A new era began. It was from these very roots that the crime leaders realized that they could no longer operate under the methods and techniques of the past. They now began to cast aside their former traits — flashy automobiles, operation of pretentious clubs, and the wearing of fancy, glaring clothing which had previously symbolized their particular breed. They now adopted the atmosphere of the ordinary, distinguished businessman and became prominent civic leaders. Next, organization leaders devised plans for a tremendous conspiracy — to create the greatest worldwide criminal cartel ever to exist within the geographical boundaries of a nation. They formalized the most unique organizational structure that has ever been developed before or since. Even though it sometimes resembled the operational

---

27. *Ibid.*
28. *Ibid.*

structure of a large legitimate corporation (29), it was so complex that it created a very distinctive buffer between each layer of operation and made it virtually impossible to identify the boss or bosses of the system (30). This new organization was designed to handle every known type of criminal enterprise from murder, blackmail, extortion, and importation of narcotics to the "ten-cent bet place" on a street corner. From the profits of these activities, money channels into every imaginable form of legitimate business in our industrial and commercial complex, even to the hot dog stand on the corner of the street (31).

As this criminal cartel expanded into every mode of American life, only a limited number of men in this country ever suspected that this organization existed or that it was formed for the express purpose of controlling all crime in the United States. These few, essentially law enforcement officials, educators, and newsmen, tried to warn the public and governmental officials of this impending danger, but were pooh-poohed as "alarmists" (32). Even as late as 1959, the Director of the FBI believed that there could not exist a criminal cartel in this country. He stressed Communist subversion as the major threat to the nation (33). So while men of this caliber were taking a complacent attitude, Mafia leaders managed to cover their tracks and organizational abilities to the finest details while at the same time they knitted together the world's most powerful and well-organized criminal cartel. They had managed to bring under their control everything from the Harlem ghetto, where one who bets a dime a day on the numbers racket, to the weekend playboy who pays out fifty dollars for a woman companion for the evening.

Even though there was no overt action taken against the Mafia, all of their activities did not go unnoticed. It had been observed by

---

29. This is an ordinary organizational chart of a legitimate corporation showing the division of responsibility, delegation of authority, and coordination of activities in a company. Charts, of course, show only the formal corporate structure; they do not reveal the de facto relationships that may be even more important.
30. Task Force Report: Organized Crime. The President's Commission on Law Enforcement and Administration of Justice.
31. Salerno and Tompkins, pp. 230-31.
32. *Ibid.*, pp. 282, 287.
33. Reid, pp. 200, 278, 300, and 306.

the public and those who have attempted to deter its gradual success. Mafia leaders were seen hosting parties attended by political leaders, lawmakers, judges, and other influential figures in the world of politics. Here the mobsters cemented contracts with politicians who would pass laws or fail to pass laws in order to favor organized crime. In turn, this enabled candidates for political office to gain support either by financial contributions or by being assured of sufficient votes to win an election. The Mafia leaders were assured that their help would not be overlooked and that they would be able to continue operating without interference of any kind. With this political influence, the Mafia leaders decided to broaden their scope of power from the criminal cartel to one of legitimate businesses where its opportunity from detection was assured. This was the beginning of a second government. There was no further need for extensive expansion of criminal activities but only to utilize the profits from these activities to foster their future plans.

Many experts believe that the Cosa Nostra (formerly the Mafia) found that milking legitimate business was so profitable that it pulled more than half of its 60 billion dollar bankroll out of the traditional "dirty" operations in order to get its hooks into "clean" businesses — banks, real estate development, land investment firms, entertainment media, luxury hotels, and small businesses of all types (34).

In this new endeavor of expanding and intensifying their activities, the mob's methods ranged from highly sophisticated stock manipulations, involving tens of millions of dollars, all the way down to the most basic extortion and violence and even use of their ultimate weapon — murder. To accomplish this design, Cosa Nostra used and is still using these major infiltration techniques: bankruptcy fraud (scam and bust out), dummy association (protection), usury (shylocking), loan manipulation, labor involvement (racketeering), hijacking (insurance frauds), real estate coups, stock thefts, monopoly, reverse monopoly, investment steering, simple extortion, illegal cartels, and inplant gambling (35).

---

34. Donald Singleton, "How Organized Crime Takes Over Business," *The American Legion Magazine* (April, 1970), p. 15.
35. *Ibid.*

Everybody pays the high cost of the Cosa Nostra's ticket from the darkness of the underworld to the daylight of pretended respectability. The cost can be measured in dollars and cents and in human misery. The cost can also be measured in higher taxes. If the Cosa Nostra paid taxes on the millions it makes, every citizens tax bill would be reduced. Profits can be measured in the thousands of needless bankruptcies resulting from scam operations, in which the mob takes over a successful business, quickly milks it dry of every drop of stock, assets and credits, leaving behind a bankrupt company and a stack of unpaid bills. It can be measured in higher insurance rates for everybody — the rates go up a little every year because of Cosa Nostra — arranged stock pilfering and hijacking frauds. It can be measured in lower wages for tens of thousands of workers who are trapped in sweetheart contracts between Cosa Nostra controlled unions and Cosa Nostra controlled companies. And it can be measured in higher price tags on all kinds of consumer goods — a one cent increase in the cost of a loaf of bread because of syndicate controlled trucking monopoly, or a ten dollar increase in the cost of a new car because of payroll padding by a subcontractor (36).

As a result of the overall Cosa Nostra operations, investigators estimate that the syndicate's annual intake is at least 60 billion dollars. Sixty billion dollars is almost incomprehensible to most people. Reduced to more understandable terms, 60 billion dollars is more than the total combined yearly sales of General Motors, Ford Motors, General Electric, International Business Machines, United States Steel, and DuPont (37). But this does not produce an accurate picture of the Cosa Nostra's worth, because the Cosa Nostra's money is "freer" than the money taken in by legitimate corporations. The mob pays very little, if any, taxes; it does not adhere to antitrust laws; it answers to no stockholders; it has no internal labor problems; and perhaps most important of all, during periods of recession and "tight" money, it has almost limitless source of capital funds from its criminal loan-sharking and gambling operations to expand its legitimate business operations, especially increasing plant assets and equipment. Because of its

36. *Ibid.*
37. *Ibid.*

alarming growth, business organizations and government agencies have begun working hand-in-hand in an effort to plan an attack on their common enemy organized crime (38).

Now the reader can understand some of the plans and designs of this powerful and destructive organization, determined to control and subvert by any means possible the government and people of the United States. Therefore consider the operational structure that affords maximum efficiency. Investigators today have identified between 3,000 and 5,000 individuals as members of the Cosa Nostra (LCN). Some authorities estimate the overall manpower at 3,000; others consider the 5,000 figure as merely the visible tip of a very deep iceberg. LCN members represent the inner core of organized crime. However, this inner core (LCN members), works in concert with other nonmember criminals or syndicates. By including this latter group of nonmember LCN-affiliated racketeers and taking into account their control of political machines, labor unions, businesses, and other types of organizations, the manpower leverage of this nation's criminal conglomerate is estimated at several hundred thousand strong (39).

LCN members belong to basic operating units or "families," of which there are currently twenty-four within the United States. The "president" of each family unit is the Boss, whose dual responsibility is to maintain order and maximize profits. His authority within his family is almost absolute; he may be overruled only by the "Commission," which is usually comprised of twelve members, selected from the bosses of the more powerful families. The Commission is the ultimate authority on organizational and jurisdictional disputes; it serves as a combination legislature, supreme court, board of directors, and arbitration panel.

Each Boss has access to a *consigliere* or counselor, a staff man who often is an elder member of the family and whose advice and judgment are sought and respected. On the same level as the consigliere is an Underboss, who acts as buffer or insulator between the Boss and the rest of the family. He collects

---

38. *Deskbook on Organized Crime,* pp. 4-5.
39. *Ibid.,* p. 5.

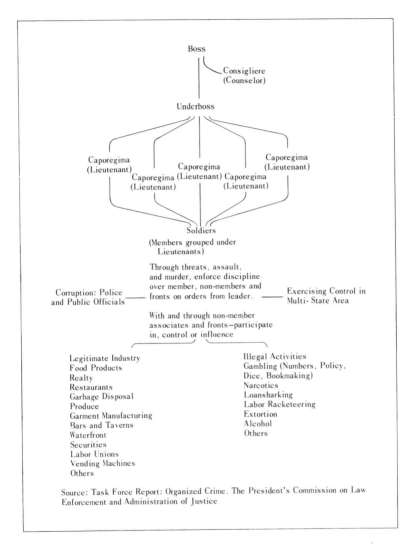

Boss

Consigliere
(Counselor)

Underboss

Caporegima
(Lieutenant)

Caporegima

Caporegima
(Lieutenant)

Caporegima (Lieutenant)  Caporegima
(Lieutenant)              (Lieutenant)

Soldiers
(Members grouped under
Lieutenants)

Through threats, assault,
and murder, enforce discipline
over member, non-members and
fronts on orders from leader.

Corruption: Police
and Public Officials

Exercising Control in
Multi- State Area

With and through non-member
associates and fronts—participate
in, control or influence

Legitimate Industry
Food Products
Realty
Restaurants
Garbage Disposal
Produce
Garment Manufacturing
Bars and Taverns
Waterfront
Securities
Labor Unions
Vending Machines
Others

Illegal Activities
Gambling (Numbers, Policy,
Dice, Bookmaking)
Narcotics
Loansharking
Labor Racketeering
Extortion
Alcohol
Others

Source: Task Force Report: Organized Crime. The President's Commission on Law
Enforcement and Administration of Justice

Figure 5. Since organized crime does not have or maintain an organizational chart per se, investigators of organized crime have compiled sufficient documentation to formulate a chart outlining the basic structure of its organization which identifies its chain of command like that of a typical Mafia family.

information for the Boss, relays messages and instructions from him. The position of the Underboss is analogous to that of an executive vice-president.

Directly below the Underboss are the *caporegimes* or lieutenants, analogous to plant supervisors or sales managers. They serve either as buffers between top men and lower level personnel or as chiefs of various operational areas of the family. Typically, each lieutenant has one or more associates carrying orders, information, and money to the soldiers or "buttonmen" who are attached to his sphere of operation and are the front-line managers of the criminal cartel. They may operate various enterprises; partnerships between one another or between themselves and higher-ups are common practice.

Soldiers employ a large number of street-level personnel who are not family members. They bear the "nitty-gritty" of the criminal enterprise by performing such tasks as taking bets, driving trucks, or working in legitimate businesses.

Though there are no written rules, standards, or procedures, except the unwritten role of *"Omerta"* (40), these matters are understood and govern the relationship among themselves as well as other family members. Enforcers are assigned to each family to maintain organizational integrity among its members by utilizing force or murder. Thus organized crime is a confederation of families, with each family so structured that the loss of even its leader will not destroy its continuity in operations (41).

Since organized crime now considers the business sphere of American life as its major industry, we can now see how it has advanced with this era of sophistication, automation, and computerization. Today's activities within the field of business mandate an individual to accumulate expertise, based upon technical knowledge and skill, to handle the operations of these expanding enterprises. Therefore, observers of this phenomenon speculate that bosses of organized crime realize that they are not

---

40. *Omerta* – a word utilized by the Mafia to mean in general terms, "Golden silence" or "Talk and you die." For the modern Mafia, terror, not the concept denoted by the time-honored word, has achieved a simplicity of operation that continues to create something even more time-honored than a word: profit. (Reid, p. 7).
41. *Deskbook of Organized Crime,* p. 6.

equipped personally to handle the problems of business and finance and therefore are sending their sons to universities to learn business administration or related skills. Perhaps this need to attract additional expertise will lead to increasingly decentralized decision making within families and, in time, result in blurring the lines between members and nonmembers (42).

Not only does the LCN need individuals which have expertise but also those with ability to handle and control the incredible financial resources of organized crime which supplies more than enough capital to penetrate and exploit legitimate business and provide an abundant slush fund for crime's lobby of corruption in such a way that it will continue to reap their ultimate goal — profit.

The ability and finesse of Cosa Nostra to manage this lobby fund is considered its critical weapon of political power and control. Through payoffs to legislators, mayors, judges, police, and other officials, the underworld is able to operate under a political umbrella of official inaction or even encouragement. This is a must in their industry, as it is axiomatic that where organized crime flourishes so also does public corruption. This lobbying is directed at federal, state, and local officials, and other agencies of government. The objective is to neuralize law enforcement by having their hands tied by a paid politician. As the President's Commission on Law Enforcement and Administration of Justice commented, "What can the public do if no one investigates the investigators, and the political figures are neutralized by their alliance with organized crime? Anyone reporting corrupt activities may merely be telling his story to the corrupted. . ." (43).

So important is political power to organized crime that each family designates a member to act as a corrupter. Among the fruits of the corrupters' efforts are judges who hand suspended sentences to major racketeers even though found guilty by juries (44), anticrime legislation bottled up in committee (45), police who

---

42. *Ibid.*
43. *Deskbook on Organized Crime,* p. 7.
44. John L. McClellan, "Weak Link in Our War On the Mafia," *Reader's Digest* (March, 1970), pp. 56-59. (Cases cited on pages 35-38 of this article).
45. "Opposition is Assured for Any Crime Bill," *Omaha World Herald* (March 16, 1970), p. 20.

look the other way (46), a trial judge conspiring with a prosecutor to obstruct justice (47), officials awarding lucrative contracts to LCN businesses (48), and the appointment of Mafia associates within political offices (49), while in the field of industry and commercial enterprises the corrupter is utilized to take control of such businesses as Murray Packing Company, New York (50); R. N. Landon Construction Company, White Plains, New York (51); and Kennedy International Airport, New York (52). There are literally hundred of citable known incidents of the Mafia's involvement in every sphere of business, but these should be sufficient to emphasize the dangers of organized crime in America.

If organized crime is so ubiquitous, why is it not more visible or more apparent? Because of this nebulous quality, some would have us believe that LCN is a myth, a figment of overactive imagination. Unfortunately, the skeptics seem more concerned with scoring debating points than examining reality.

Reality reveals that organized crime labors hard at keeping itself out of the public eye. The status quo is valued, for rocking the boat will elicit unwarranted attention by citizens, the press, and police. Criminal operations thereby suffer. This is why each family has an enforcer who minimizes bloody internal flare-ups by meting out discipline; this is why the corrupter is so valuable; this is why the organized underworld mounts public relations campaigns to throw the public off guard; this is why underworld higher-ups generally lead unostentatious lives and attempt to assume a mantle of respectability through their business connections or other means; this is why the underworld kingpins like to hear the public and officials say that they do not believe in the existence of organized crime.

---

46. Salerno and Tompkins, p. 246 (Cites stories of police payoff).
47. McClellan, p. 61.
48. Sandy Smith, "The Mob Finds a Patsy in a Mayor's Circle," *Saturday Evening Post* (January 5, 1968), pp. 44-50. (Story of James L. Marcus, former Commissioner of Water, Gas and Electricity, New York, N. Y.).
49. Christopher S. Wren and Margaret English, "Murder New Jersey Style," *Look* (March 10, 1970), pp. 43-47.
50. Salerno and Tompkins, pp. 235-36; Singleton, p. 16.
51. Singleton, p. 17.
52. John N. Mitchell, "Mob Controls Big Airport," *Omaha World Herald* (January 24, 1970), p. 2; Singleton, p. 19.

Figure 6. This is a map compiled by investigators and presented to the President's Commission on Organized Crime showing and identifying the exact locations of major cities within the United States where the core elements of the Mafia are located and operating. Because of political involvement, the Commission was not allowed to furnish this map for public scrutiny. (From Salerno and Tompkins: *Crime Confederation.* Doubleday, New York, 1969, p. 321.)

Actually, the criminal confederation is so pervasive that it is highly probable that most U. S. adults have contributed, knowingly and unknowingly, to the coffers of crime by donating to charities or foundations established by the underworld; patronizing hotels, restaurants, or dry cleaning establishments operated by LCN; purchasing automobile insurance from racketeer insurers; using vending machines installed by a syndicate; voting for a politician secretly obligated to organized crime; renting an apartment or conducting business in a building owned by a mob-controlled real estate concern; wagering with the local bookie, who may be a nice guy but none the less is at the end of a string pulled by organized crime.

Those who doubt the presence of organized crime in their communities should ask themselves, "Has anyone ever looked?" Just as the discovery of oil usually requires considerable drilling, unearthing organized crime involves diligent digging. Skeptics should ask themselves, "Have local police established units to investigate organized crime?" They should ask themselves, "How does the local bookie service his many accounts or how does he obtain 'the line' or odds?" or "How does he receive race results so quickly that no one can past post him?" or "How is he the recipient of a massive nationwide flow of information?" They should ask themselves, "How does merchandise written off as inventory shrinkage appear in retail outlets thousands of miles away?" They should ask themselves many such questions and their answers will reveal the wide-ranging operation of criminal cartel deeply embedded in the fabric of American life (53).

Now is the time for all Americans, ordinary citizens, business-men, and politicians to open their eyes and observe what has been occurring and listen to the warnings of dedicated men who are expounding the rise of organized crime within the United States. In a speech very recently before the United States Senate, John McClellan, Chairman of the Sub-committee on Criminal Laws and Procedures, said:

> Legitimate business is another area into which organized crime has begun most recently and widely to extend its influence. In most cities, it now dominates the fields of jukeboxes and vending machine distribution. Laundry services, liquor and beer distribution, nightclubs, food wholesaling, record manufacturing, the garment industry, and a host of other legitimate lines of endeavor have been invaded and taken over. The Special Committee to Investigate Organized Crime in Interstate Commerce, under the leadership of Senator Estes Kefauver, noted in 1952 that the following industries had been invaded: advertising, amusement, appliances, automobile, baking, ballrooms, bowling alleys, banking, basketball, boxing, cigarette distribution, coal, communications, construction, drug stores, electrical equipment, florists, food, football, garment, gas, hotels, import-export, insurance, jukebox, laundry, liquor, loan, news service, newspapers, oil, paper products, radio, real estate, restaurants, scrap shipping, steel surplus, television, theaters, and transportation (54).

Today we hear shouts — Robbery! Rape! Murder! — and many other cries that are considered prime evils of an orderly society.

---

53. *Deskbook on Organized Crime*, p. 9.
54. *Ibid.*

Yet have we realized or looked at what may be behind this surge of crime in order to gain insight into why it might exist? As if organized crime, in its own unique ways, did not generate enough problems for business and society, consider the correlation between the astounding economic and political successes of the criminal confederation and the explosive surfacing of street crime in recent years. Though the organized underworld certainly is not responsible for all street crime, LCN makes a substantial contribution, directly or indirectly, to such violence. One of the strongest statements in this regard was made by the Director of the National Council on Crime and Delinquency: "Almost every bit of crime has some link to organized crime" (55).

Strangely enough, organized crime's indirect link to street crime is the most serious. The "shining" record of the underworld serves as a powerful magnet by attracting numerous fence-sitters to a life of crime. As a consultant to the President's Commission observed:

> For good or for ill, the law and its failure teach. People know when crime pays. Kids in the slums see the cop on the beat take money. They know the pusher seldom gets caught, and his wholesaler is virtually never touched. They learn this lesson better than any middle class values taught in the schools from which they drop out. This implication of the failure of our legal system to hold those who openly flaunt our laws accountable undermines the entire system. Not only is crime not deterred, it is indirectly promoted (56).

Another crime authority reports that a group of youths in a large city "once told me that they saw life in their community as racket figures with public officials running the world" (57). Also the President's Commission concluded that "Cosa Nostra leaders and their racketeering allies preach a sermon all too many Americans heed: The government is for sale; lawlessness is the road to wealth; honesty is a pitfall and morality a trap for suckers" (58).

In short, all too often the LCN has demonstrated that crime pays and pays handsomely. Even lower echelon Nostra personnel can be millionaires. This fact is not lost upon today's youth. As one observer commented, "Racketeers are often the heroes of the

---

55. "The Conglomerate of Crime," *Time* (August 22, 1969), pp. 17-27.
56. *Deskbook on Organized Crime*, p. 13.
57. *Ibid.*
58. *Ibid.*

young persons in deprived areas" (59).

More directly bearing on street crime is the recruitment activity of LCN. According to testimony, racketeers have been known to train youths in lower-level crimes as preparation for entry into the ranks of the criminal elite. LCN sponsors burglaries and hijackings – even bank robberies (60). Another LCN contribution to everyday crime is theft-to-order operations. This involves old-fashioned cattle rustling in order to supply meat for syndicate restaurants, and hijacking valuable merchandise to supply racketeer-controlled retailing operations. Attorney General Mitchell has said, "When you read of housebreakings, shoplifting and industrial thefts, you should realize that organized crime provides a major network for the disposal of stolen goods" (61).

Now that we have dealt with the aspects of organized crime and are able to understand the inner workings, final purpose and goals within the American society, we can consider what each and every American can do to assist in the ultimate defeat of organized crime. First, we must look at organized crime from the standpoint that it can be defeated, but a successful war against it requires that we recognize crime as an enemy of society. We must anticipate that organized crime is as dedicated to eventual and ultimate control of our country through subversive and forcible tactics as certain Communists are in their design for world domination. Second, we must make it known to each and every person in the United States that Cosa Nostra and organized crime do exist. Third, we must understand that organized crime will not disappear by itself and armies of police alone will not solve the problem.

Americans must take the initiative and exert some overt action against the crime threat. To correct the conditions in which organized crime thrives, citizens must stop, knowingly or unknowingly, cooperating with criminals. This may mean uncomfortable changes in behavior for many people. We will have to stop buying smuggled, tax-free cigarettes. We will have to seek legal outlets for our gambling instincts. We will have to stop betting with the bookmakers and lottery operators. Businessmen will have to give up services of "labor consultants" who earn their

59. *Ibid.*
60. *Ibid.*, p. 14.
61. *Ibid.*

fees by victimizing workers. We will have to come forth and give evidence without fear of reprisal and testify to our knowledge of organized criminal activities. We will have to give full faith and support to law enforcement officials who have dedicated themselves to the general welfare and protection of every citizen's life and property. We will have to force the complacent politicians to take an interest in the citizen and support of the laws that will curtail organized crime. The citizen will have to be willing to sacrifice some of the rights that he feels he deserves under the constitution, such as liberalization of statutes involving wiretapping and eavesdropping and broader rights of search and seizure.

Is it not better to sacrifice some of these privileges to be protected or later become subjected to the complete control and domination of an organization that will enslave society? Do we have the courage for this kind of individual moral, political, and intellectual honesty? The ultimate choice belongs to the citizen. What are we going to do? Will it be apathy or action? If we choose apathy, organized crime will continue to grow. If we take action, organized crime will fail. If we decide on action, it must be in the right direction and swift, for the syndicates are alert and will marshal their political and public relations muscle in an attempt to defeat the new threat. If organized crime is successful in this countermove and manages to brand all our attempts to fight crime as unfair, un-American and unconstitutional, crime then will win, growing faster and stronger than ever before to become not just a major factor in the American way of life, but the way of life. Victory is not at all certain, even if we choose wisely, but no war against a determined enemy was ever a sure thing. Losing would be no disgrace. The only disgrace would be not to fight.

The majority of the law enforcement agencies within the United States have begun to realize that there is a major threat to the American way of life from organized crime, and they have begun to fight it. In the last decade, the nation's Law Enforcement agencies have mounted an increasingly vigorous assault against the estimated 5,000 Cosa Nostra who dominate organized crime in America. Yet, despite some significant successes in prosecution, President Nixon told Congress last April that "we have not substantially impeded the growth and power of organized syndicates. Not a single one of the 24 Cosa Nostra families has been destroyed. They are more firmly entrenched than ever before" (62).

Why is this, and what has caused this ineffective fight against organized crime? This disheartening routing by the enemy is due in significant part to the shocking judicial leniency in sentencing convicted Mafiosi leaders. Consider the following instances:

*Chicago:* Rocco Potenzo, right hand man of Mafia Ross Sam "Momo" Ciancana. Internal Revenue agents arrested Potenzo for feloniously operating without Federal liquor licenses under the names of front men. Maximum sentence could have been 15 years in jail and a $10,000 fine. Upon conviction, Potenzo was fined $1,000 by the judge trying the case and given no jail time.

*Pennsylvania:* Walter Joseph Plopi, Mafia corrupter charged and convicted of bribery to operate a gambling establishment. Maximum sentence was a year in jail. Plopi was convicted and fined $250. He was given back the $300 bribe money so when he walked out of court he was $50 richer than when he walked in.

*California:* Jimmy "The Weasel" Fratianno, West Coast Enforcer for the Mafia. Charged with swindling truck drivers working on a Federal contract hauling dirt for the interstate highway project. Convicted in court of 16 counts of conspiracy and filing false statements which could have netted him 80 years in prison, he was only fined $10,000, no jail time.

*New York:* Anthony Corallo, a Capo of one of the five New York Mafia families. He had been convicted twice by the same judge for bribery and loansharking. Sentenced to pull a little over 5 years out of a total 10 years he could have received.

*New England:* Louis Taglianetti, a soldier in Patriarca crime family. Convicted of income tax evasion where he could have received a 5 year sentence. However, he only received 7 months. Ironically, for the ordinary citizen committing the same offense the sentence averaged 10 months.

*New York:* John Lomnardozzi, brother of a Capo in New York's Gambino Mafia family. Charged with four separate felony counts. Convicted on all four counts. Sentenced to five years in jail when he could have received 28 years.

---

62. McClellan, p. 56.

*New England:* Jerry Angiulo, Underboss in Patriarca Family who controls the Boston Syndicate. Charged with assault of a Federal officer where he could have received 3 years. Sentenced to 30 days in jail.

These are but a few of the many cases where judges have netted out very minimal sentences because they are allowed by state statutes to exercise their own discretion in handing out sentences upon conviction (63). It is this type of action by judges throughout the United States that has caused the National Crime Commission in 1967 to make the following statement: "There must be some kind of supervision over those trial judges who, because of corruption, political considerations or lack of knowledge, tend to mete out light sentences in cases involving organized crime management personnel" (64).

Because of the power and influence that the Cosa Nostra has established over its four decades of operations within the United States and the leniency that it has received from our legal system, there are recommendations being presented to Congress for adoption in order to prevent the continued expansion of organized crime. Such recommendations are being presented by Senators Sam J. Ervin (D.,N.C.), James B. Allen (D.,Ala.), Roman L. Hruska (R.,Nebr.), and John L. McClellan (D.,Ark.) under the Organized Crime Control Act of 1970. This bill will include the following provisions:

(Senate Bill #30)

> This bill provides for both prosecutor appeals and special sentences for habitual offenders and members of organized criminal con-spiracies. Under its provisions, the trial judge would, after a pre-sentence hearing at which the offender would have the right to call witnesses, cross-examine the government's witnesses and be informed of the substance of any information the judge might rely on. Upon finding that the offender had two prior felony convictions, or had committed a felony as a part of a conspiracy with three or more others to engage in a pattern of criminal conduct, the judge could order a sentence up to 30 years (65).

This is, in fact, the cornerstone of the federal government's mounting campaign against organized crime. President Nixon has

---

63. McClellan, pp. 56-59.
64. *Ibid.,* p. 57.
65. McClellan, p. 61.

given his support to this bill by stating:

> Through large-scale target investigations, we believe we can obtain
> prosecutions that will imprison the leaders, paralyze the
> administrators, frighten the street workers and eventually, paralyze
> the whole organized-crime syndicate in any one particular city. This
> strategy can succeed — but only if the court record of the past ten
> years can be reversed (66).

To combat the elements of organized crime, perhaps some steps
of immediate action are necessary.

*First:* More active involvement by local law enforcement
agencies to organize an effective Intelligence section within their
departments that will accumulate and document vital information
concerning any alleged or actual operations of organized crime
should be the rule.

*Second:* Federal and state laws should be established to
organize a specialized Criminal Investigative Agency in each area
of the United States with compulsory standards and training in the
area of organized crime.

*Third:* All information obtained from investigative agencies
regarding organized crime should be by law forwarded to the Law
Enforcement Intelligence Unit for correlation and overall statistics
of organized crime.

*Fourth:* A comprehensive computerized Data System on all
known or suspected persons engaged in organized criminal
activities should be established and maintained.

*Fifth:* A liaison with the Crime Prevention and Control section
of the Chamber of Commerce of the United States should be
coordinated and maintained in order that known organized
criminal leaders, associates and their methods of operations can be
disseminated to the businesses for their protection from infiltration of organized crime.

*Sixth:* There must be instruction incorporated into our
academic structure in the high schools, colleges, and universities.
In high school, in civic and government classes students must be
made aware that organized crime does exist and affects every
mode of our society. In colleges and universities a specialized
course could be adopted under the title of "Organized Crime," to

---

66. *Ibid.*

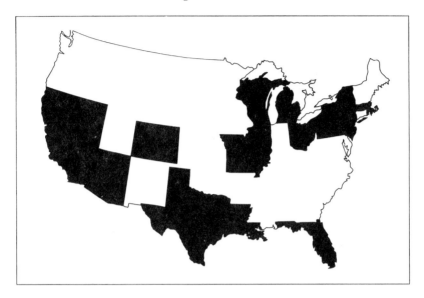

Figure 7. Since the map as presented in Figure 6 was not acceptable for public scrutiny, the Commission prepared a compromise version of this map. Instead of showing the exact location of the core elements of the Mafia, this map shows the general areas within the United States where the Mafia has penetrated and is maintaining its area of operations. (From Salerno and Tompkins: *Crime Confederation.* Doubleday, New York, 1969, p. 323.)

be taught to Business, Law Enforcement, Public Administration, Psychology, and Sociology majors as well as to students in other related fields. This course could cover the origin and development of the Mafia, its development and penetration into the United States, its methods and techniques employed to subvert and corrupt the business sphere and law enforcement and politicians within the United States, its sociological and psychological effects upon the American society and the ways and means to combat the further penetration of organized crime into our way of life. Only through comprehensive educational achievements can one understand the complexity of organized crime and its ultimate effects within our democratic society. It is with the younger generation that the hope of defeating organized crime exists.

There are many other possible solutions, but these must be worked out through the complete cooperation of all entities: businessmen, politicians, law enforcement officials, and most of all, the citizens.

# Chapter 10

# THE USE OF FORCE

## HISTORICAL ASPECTS

T HE over-use of force, or perhaps force to any degree, so commonly referred to by today's public as "police brutality," is not relatively new to the American scene. Policing bodies have been plagued throughout history by critics as to their methods of quelling disturbances and the apprehension of criminals, whether it be by group or individual force.

One of the earliest examples of force was in 1786 during Shay's Rebellion. The state militia was called to quell rebel farmers who had gathered in front of the courthouse at Springfield, Massachusetts. A mob of about 600 persons, composed of small property owners and farmers revolting against their creditors and against high taxes collected in Massachusetts, had threatened the Supreme Court and prevented the court from allowing the foreclosure of farms and the imprisonment of debtors. A mob of this size was of course too large to be handled by a constable with a handful of men. The state militia, under the command of Major General Benjamin Lincoln, was able to subdue the rebels by the use of group tactics. Lincoln's men, armed with rifles and fixed bayonets, formed a wedge-type riot formation to move the rebels away from the courthouse. Although for the most part the wedge-type formation worked successfully to move the farmers from the courthouse, a few were shot and beaten by the militia because of strong resistance encountered.

During the 1800's most of the law enforcement in the majority of the United States was handled by local sheriffs. Force to these men was usually either at a minimum or maximum. The sheriff or his deputy would ask an unwanted man to leave town. If he did, the only force used would be verbal. If he did not, he would either be put in jail or shot.

In 1835, a group known as the Texas Rangers was organized. These men were the first form of state police. Dealing with cattle rustlers, outlaws, Indians, and marauding Mexicans from across the border, the use of force by these men was handled quite similarly to that of the local sheriffs. The Texas Rangers was a very well-organized group, as well as a very respected group, even to the present time.

The year of the great railroad strikes was 1877. Never before in America had labor disputes been so widespread, so damaging to commerce, or so marked by violence. Between the onset of the strikes of 1877 and the close of the Chicago railway in 1894, railroad strikes, boycotts, and strike threats became common (67). The federal government at this time was constantly trying to suppress these strikes. The strikes often got out of hand before the government was called in. The usual goal of intervention was to halt the strikes and to restore law, order, and regular railway service as quickly as possible. Usually the government agents could stop the strikes with a minimal degree of force. However, many times railroad workers had to be taken into custody for interfering with the government.

In 1905 there were more strikes. These, however, were statewide coal strikes. During this time the Pennsylvania State Police came into being. Armed with clubs, hand guns, and rifles, the police stopped many of the coal miners from destroying community property. The Pennsylvania State Police were accused of strike-breaking by the public, but force was at a minimum, and the miners went back to work.

A good example of an excessive amount of group force can be depicted .by the Bonus Expeditionary Force of May, June, and July of 1932. The Bonus Law of 1924 had given every veteran a certificate that was payable in 1945. The veterans, because they were hungry, homeless and out of work because of the depression, wanted the bonus paid immediately. Coming from all areas of the United States, some 10,000 Bonus marchers went to Washington, D. C. to bring pressure on the Senate to pass the bill (68). Crowds of veterans stood on the Capitol steps, marched around the building and visited senators. For eight weeks the Bonus marchers patiently and painfully camped in the open extemporaneous

67. G. G. Eggert, *Railroad Labor Disputes,* p. 155.
68. John Henry Bartlett, *The Bonus March and the New Deal,* p. 1.

shelters to wait for the outcome of their demands. These destitute ex-servicemen petitioned their government for food and care, as well as the Bonus in a time of distress only to find that a federal policy of no-aid had been invoked against them.

No-federal-aid-for-the-poor  —  this was the verdict of the government. "Aid to anyone at this time is virtually not a financially sound idea," was the statement of President Herbert Hoover. The Bonus Marcher's hope for aid had been quelled, and now their future seemed doomed.

Up until this time, the local police agency had kept the Bonus Marchers in line, but now since the bill had been rejected, Secretary of War Huntly, on a perfunctory command from President Herbert Hoover, the Commander-in-Chief, called out a contingent of the United States Army under the command of General MacArthur to disperse the marchers (69).

This swift movement of the marchers from Washington by police, cavalry, infantry and armor, proved very disheartening to the majority of the public. During the evacuation two unarmed veterans, William J. Hushka and Eric Carlson, were shot to death. A nine-month-old baby died from gas when a passing soldier threw a gas grenade into a house. Three dead and many wounded — this to the public was an excessive use of force by the government.

Although law and order cannot be maintained without some loss of individual freedom, the methods imposed on citizens during the late twenties and early thirties really got out of hand. During this time the so-called "third degree" came into effect.

Policemen in their eagerness to detect crime and to apprehend and bring criminals to justice sometimes overlooked the importance of the government function as a safeguard of personal liberty.

## DEADLY FORCE

Deadly force is that force likely to cause serious physical injury or death. The firing of a weapon, except on the range during practice, should always be considered a deadly force even though

---

69. *Ibid.,* p. 53.

the intent of the officer was merely to frighten or to sound an alarm. Once the weapon has been fired, the officer has used potentially deadly force. This would normally include the use of the baton or nightstick, chemical mace, and most "come along" or submission devices. However, these can very easily be utilized in such a manner as to also constitute deadly force.

Without exception, the cardinal rule emphasized by all of the law enforcement agencies is that an officer may use only that amount of force, either deadly or nondeadly, which is reasonably necessary for the accomplishment of his mission. Any unnecessary use of force, or unreasonable harrassment, places the officer outside the protection of the law and subjects him to either disciplinary action by his department or liability through the court system.

Every now and then a police officer is criticized in the press for excessive use of force or discharge of his firearm. He is usually charged with poor judgment or with exceeding his authority. At the same time, his chief is often criticized for not having properly trained the man in his responsibilities. It is charged that the department does not have an adequate statement of policy as a guide to the officers in these important matters. Actually, most departments do have a statement of policy covering the discharge of firearms by officers. Also, as for training, almost without exception, a training course in which the practical work is always accompanied by a discussion of the circumstances under which force and weapons should and should not be used. Still, we frequently see articles, similar to the example cited earlier, charging officers with indiscriminate shooting and describing them as being "trigger happy." Everyone will agree that the decision to shoot someone is the most momentous decision a police officer can make. Once the trigger is pulled, the action is irreversible; the decision, irrevocable. So, it is of paramount importance to have a clear-cut statement of policy to guide the men in making such decisions.

## RESPONSIBILITIES

One of the primary responsibilities which the chief of any law enforcement agency owes, not only to those officers under his jurisdiction, but to those people to whom he is responsible for safety and protection, is the formulation and promulgation of clear and concise policies concerning the expected actions of those officers in his department (70). One of the most vital areas of policy necessity is that of the use of force in the performance of assigned duties. The chief executive must establish these policies, of course, with the concurrence and approval of the government which he represents, to insure backing in their implimentation and enforcement. These policies must be in such detail as to furnish adequate guidance to those expected to comply with their provisions but not so minute, or filled with trifles, as to stiffle *any* initiative or freedom of action by the officer. Also, these policies must be constantly updated as decisions of the courts and trends in law enforcement change. Although there are few universally accepted guidelines which law enforcement agencies follow in formulating policies covering situations where particular types and degrees of force are called for and authorized, several areas have been found to be fairly similar.

## FIREARMS

By far the biggest area of controversy, as far as the use of force is concerned, is in the area of firearms utilization. Most police departments have general orders or departmental directives furnishing fairly specific guidelines for the use of a weapon at a fleeing person guilty of a misdemeanor. A Baltimore Police Department directive comments on this thusly, "Under no circumstances shall a member of the department shoot at a person who is running away to avoid arrest on a misdemeanor charge, as the law recognizes that it is better to allow a misdemeanant to escape than to take his life. Members must always bear in mind, 'When in doubt, Don't Fire,' (Cardinal Rule)" (71).

The General Order issued by the Chief of Police of Kansas City concerning the discharge of firearms is fairly representative of most other departments and is quoted as follows:

70. Kansas City Police Department Rules.
71. Baltimore Police Department Code of Rules, *Firearms,* Rule #3, p. 4.

A. An officer may discharge his firearms for any of the following purposes.
   1. To defend himself from death or serious injury.
   2. To defend another person unlawfully attacked from death or serious injury.
   3. To perfect the arrest or prevent the escape, after notice, when all other means fail, of a person whom the officer has reasonable grounds to believe has committed a felony.
   4. To prevent a felony involving force, surprise or violence.
   5. To kill a dangerous animal, or to kill an animal so badly injured that humanity requires that it be destroyed to prevent further suffering.
   6. When an attempt is made to rescue by violence a prisoner who is in lawful custody of an officer.
B. Nothing in this order shall restrict the discharge of firearms on a firearms range or while participating in an authorized training mission (72).

The Baltimore Police Department adds one additional purpose as follows: "to give alarm or to call assistance when *no* other means can be used" (73).

Another requirement laid down in the majority of directives is the submission, in writing, of a report whenever a firearm is discharged by a member of the department in line of duty, giving full particulars, except when it is used on the range or while participating in an authorized training mission.

One situation, although not specifically mentioned in available departmental directives, which must be considered by an officer before he fires his weapon is that of the possibility of injury or death to innocent persons not only from direct fire but from ricocheting and "returning to earth" type bullets. Several of the departments indicate that their guidance to officers is that if an innocent person may be hurt, withhold firing except in the actual protection of *life*.

## Moving Vehicles

Another area of constant problem to law enforcement agencies

---

72. Kansas City Police Department memorandum #67-37, *Discharge of Firearms*, Paragraph III, (Kansas City, Missouri: 1967).
73. Baltimore Police Department Rule #3, *Firearms.*

is in that of firing at a moving vehicle or when the officer is in a moving vehicle. Again, although not specifically mentioned in directives, most police departments generally agree that it is best to attempt to apprehend the individual through the use of police communications media and cooperative police work, if possible. The danger to innocent persons from unexpended or ricocheting bullets or out of control vehicles usually far outweighs any justifications for high speed chases and exchange of gunfire. However, a car should not become a sanctuary for a criminal at whom an officer is otherwise justified in firing if the officer is close enough to fire accurately, if the shot will likely be effective in stopping the car and/or suspect and most important of all, if the danger to innocent persons can be basically eliminated.

It is felt that, almost without exception, all departments stress and insist on compliance with the guidance set down by the Baltimore department — "When in doubt, Don't Shoot."

## THE BATON

The baton or nightstick is an effective weapon for the police officer skilled in its proper use (74). The police officer who knows how to use his baton with propriety performs his duties with an extra measure of confidence and with the advantage of effective counterattack over the aggressive lawbreaker. The regulation baton has durability and is designed to meet all the requirements for police service *without* weighting or leading.

A sharp blow to the collar muscles, shoulders, or biceps is very effective. A well-aimed blow to the kneecap, shin bone, or upper leg can end a fight quickly by paralyzing nerves without causing permanent injury to the adversary.

Blows to the body with the baton are designed primarily to paralyze a muscle or nerve center. Jabs to the stomach are intended to take the suspect's breath away. Mild state of shock usually results to the victim in either jabs or blows.

When used correctly, the baton is an effective weapon against punches, kicks, bottles or other similar attacks or weapons. It is

---

74. Charlotte Police Department Training Bulletin #7.

useful in the application of "come alongs" and may be employed in many crowd control situations.

## MACE

Mace, which has almost universally replaced tear gas, especially in the larger cities, is designed to enable officers to perform their duties in a more efficient and humane manner when dealing with persons who intend to do bodily harm to themselves, other persons, or to the police officer (75). If used properly, the chemical Mace will reduce the risk of injury to the officer or other persons.

The chemical Mace may be used in any situation where it becomes necessary for an officer to subdue or bring under physical restraint any person while the officer is performing his official duties, regardless of whether or not the officer is making an arrest. However, once a violent person has been subdued and brought under control, there is no further justification to use the chemical Mace against the person.

The Charlotte Police Department directive very accurately covers its use and reads, in part, as follows:

> The Chemical Mace may be used in situations where physical resistance is encountered when making an arrest; where physical combat is imminent or to stop physical combat; when subdueing violently insane persons or in any situation as a self defense weapon. The use of the Chemical Mace protects the attacker, as well as the officer, against injury. Good judgment should prevail in its use as in the use of any other device. Do not overuse it. Do not use it where lesser means will accomplish the objective.
>
> The most effective use of the Mace is a well-aimed, one-second burst. A one-second burst will attain a range of approximately (15) feet, the maximum range of the Chemical Mace. The Chemical Mace projects a shotgun patter of heavy droplets of a specially prepared liquid base solution and a highly refined form of CN, strongly irritating to eyes, nose, and skin.
>
> Aim at the face of the attacker, the eyes being the "bull's eye." Upon facial contact the droplets release vapors of CN irritant which cause profuse tearing. At the same time the droplets wet, spread, and

---

75. Kansas City Police Department memorandum #67-10, *Use of Mace.*

cling to the skin causing a burning sensation and a sense of apathy occurs in the recipient. He will be incapacitated for an average of fifteen to twenty minutes (76).

Some definitely prohibited utilizations of chemical Mace include:

1. Use as a threat to make a person comply with an officer's verbal order, when no physical violence is imminent.

2. Use against any person in retaliation for their verbal abuse of an officer.

3. Use, either actually or as a threat, to elicit information from any person.

## THE NUTCRACKER

Law enforcement agencies have for years attempted to develop an inexpensive, yet effective and relatively noninjurious device for use in restraining apprehendees. A variety of expensive hardware has been tested but the nightstick and handcuffs remained the basic tools of restraint. Now, police in Detroit think that they have the answer (77). They have developed a new ten dollar weapon known as the "nutcracker," which consists of two foot-long plastic sticks joined at one end by four short nylon cords.

Pointed at the suspect like a dowser's divining rod, the weapon works on two simple principles — speed and pressure. Before the offender can escape, or if he resists arrest, the sticks are clamped around his arm, wrist, or hand. The cords act as a hinge. If he resists, the arresting officer merely squeezes the sticks, inducing severe, immobilizing pain. Either way no permanent injury is usually inflicted because the pain will usually subdue the offender before any physical damage occurs.

The nutcracker is equally effective in mob control and dispersal. Holding onto only one stick, the patrolman swings the other like a flail. Any attempt to grab the swirling stick may result in a broken or badly bruised limb. A blow on the head can fracture a skull. Says a Detroit police official: "With six men carrying the sticks we

76. Charlotte Police Department Information Bulletin #31, *The Chemical Mace* (Charlotte, North Carolina: 1967).
77. "Nutcracker," *Time* (February 28, 1969), p. 27.

can penetrate fifty men and bust up their formation and come back out."

On the strength of Detroit's success with the instrument, Michigan state police and forty-five other municipal and county police organizations are now testing the nutcracker.

## POLICE DOGS

A K-9 squad is used at times for the following:

1. Preventive patrol, both motorized and on foot.

2. Tracking and building search. (This includes calls such as holdups, car and foot chases, purse snatches, etc.)

3. To protect police officers and other persons from injury or death.

4. To effect the arrest or prevent the escape of a convicted felon or of a person who the police officer has reasonable grounds to believe has committed a felony.

5. At the scene of riots, imminent riots, or other unruly crowd situations upon approval of the Chief of Police, Patrol Division Commander, Commander of the Special Operations Division, or the on-duty Watch Commander.

6. For special assignments when authorized by the Commander of the Special Operations Division (78).

Needless to say the utilization of dogs in situations indicated in subparagraph 5 above is usually used as a last resort. Various anti-police organizations have been able to convince many that police dog techniques are vicious, and some departments have given up their K-9 corps under public pressure. The psychological effect of even the presence of specially trained dogs in the area of mass disorder or riot conditions far outweighs the adverse public opinion generated.

## AUTHORITY FOR USE OF FORCE

The authority and responsibility for the use of force to restore order lies first with local government. Many cities have the

---

78. Kansas City Police Department General Order #68-32, *K-9 Squad* (Kansas City, Missouri: 1968).

attitude that restoring order is solely a police function. That cannot be and is not so (79)! While it is true that the police play the major role, all of the city's resources must be applied. City plans for civil disorder, such as *Procedural Instruction 68-2, Control of Civil Disorder, Kansas City, Missouri,* dated June 16, 1969, are detailed in their efforts to tie all resources into an effective force under the control of the police department. Officials from many cities, states, and the federal government have received instruction in city planning for civil disturbances at the Civil Disturbance Operations Course (SEADOC) taught by the United States Army Military Police School at Fort Gordon, Georgia. All attendees received a typed city plan which emphasizes a coordinated city effort.

All too often a city will not have sufficient resources to meet its needs in the application of force to restore order. When this is so, horizontal or inter-local arrangements can be made to a degree depending on the legal requirements of the city and state (80). Some of the arrangements which can be made are for additional police, assistance in fire fighting, use of hospitals, use of airports, and use of sanitation facilities. California has established a master law enforcement mutual aid plan. Under this plan, law enforcement officers may be transferred from outside the local area to aid in restoring order. The transferred officer is paid by his own city. State law gives him legal standing in the area to which he is transferred. Application for such assistance is made first to the county sheriff and then to regional authorities who can get help from any part of the state (81). Should a city be unable or unwilling to restore order, the state has the authority and responsibility to do so.

The first force applied by the state is the use of the state police. Normally, however, the state police are committed before the situation gets out of hand and as a means of increasing the numbers of the local police. The most potent force of state authority in the application of force is the National Guard. The trend today is toward earlier commitment of these state military

79. David J. Farmer, *Civil Disorder Control,* (Chicago, 1968), p. 1.
80. *Ibid.,* p. 14.
81. *Ibid.,* p. 19.

forces (82). This may be explained by the greater violence and duration of modern disturbances and the requirement for the police to maintain normal law and order functions. Some feel that the early and repeated use of military force is a mistake, as the use of such force results in greater demoralizing effect and reduction of the shock value of that force (83). Whatever the local feelings are, plans to call and use the National Guard must be included in the overall city plan. An aspect here is the legal standing of the guard member in relation to the police, the citizen and the courts.

The final and least called upon force is that of the federal military to include the Federalized National Guard. The authority and responsibility of the federal government depends on the requirement of necessity. More specifically, "When state authorities are unable or unwilling to maintain law and order, the use of active Army or Federalized National Guard forces in civil disturbances is based upon both Federal statutes and the U. S. Constitution's provision that the President is Commander in Chief of the Armed Forces and charged with faithful execution of the laws. The Constitution also guarantees each state a representative government and protection against invasion and domestic violence.

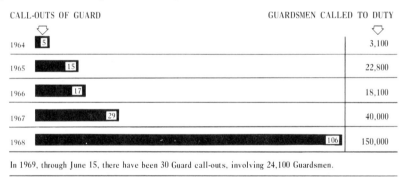

CALL-OUTS OF GUARD    GUARDSMEN CALLED TO DUTY

| Year | Call-outs | Guardsmen |
|------|-----------|-----------|
| 1964 | 5 | 3,100 |
| 1965 | 15 | 22,800 |
| 1966 | 17 | 18,100 |
| 1967 | 29 | 40,000 |
| 1968 | 106 | 150,000 |

In 1969, through June 15, there have been 30 Guard call-outs, involving 24,100 Guardsmen.

Source: National Guard Association of U.S.

Figure 8. This chart illustrates the rise in called-for services for the National Guard. (Reprinted from *U.S. News & World Report.* Copyright 1969 U. S. News & World Report, Inc.)

82. United States Army Military Police School, *A Platoon Leader's Guide for Civil Disturbance Operations,* (Fort Gordon, 1968), p. 4.
83. David J. Farmer, *Civil Disorder Control,* (Chicago, 1968), p. 4.

Further, the Fourteenth Amendment guarantees to every citizen certain constitutional privileges and immunities and equal protection of the laws" (84).

## THE APPLICATION OF FORCE

We can now turn to aspects of the actual application of force. "The guiding principle for the application of force at any time should be minimum force, consistent with mission accomplishment" (85). Because of today's mass media and of training in the subject, we have seen that the careful use of police force can prevent violence.

When it has been decided to apply a degree of force, the force commander must be guided by the fact that the suppression of violence, without undue force, is a basic policy (86). Commanders will have the problem of the soldier or police officer who internalizes the abuse heaped on him and strikes back. The individual must be made to understand that the reckless or malicious use of force may subject him to civil or criminal liability or both and that the greatest assets a control force has is its discipline, unity of purpose, and immediate response to leadership. The internalized application of force at MIT (5:30 PM newscast, November 5, 1969), which showed several police officers breaking from the organized police formation and charging the students, was a breakdown of purpose and control. It appeared that way on TV and that is the way it was reported. *Newsweek* also pointed out that the police unit as a whole displayed a great deal of restraint and purpose (87). While police officers may have a strong desire to strike out at those who vilify them, violence is not the answer. Punishment is not the job of the police officer.

Research has proven that most police departments use degrees of force adapted from the United States Army and contained in

---

84. Department of the Army Pamphlet 360-81, *To Insure Domestic Tranquility* (Washington, 1968), p. 5.
85. Department of the Army Field Manual 19-15, *Civil Disturbances and Disasters,* (Washington, 1968), p. 3-2.
86. *Ibid.,* 2-1.
87. "Go Back! Go Back!", *Newsweek* (November 17, 1969), p. 79.

Department of the Army Field Manual, 19-15, dated, March, 1968. These degrees of force are designed to accomplish the mission of restoring order with the minimum use of force. There can be no hard and fast rules concerning the application of force as situations will vary. Degrees of force enumerated in any set of regulations can be only guidelines.

The first step is to conduct a show of force. This may vary from a police squad armed with batons to a sizeable military force with bayonets and automatic weapons. It is to be noted that the goal of many rioters today is to effect a physical contact with the police; thus the show of force may not be as effective as it once was, since this is what is wanted, a force to fight with.

The next stop is the employment of riot control formations. Again, the force will vary from police with batons to troops with bayonets. Demonstrators know that if they fight, the police officers will use their batons, but that the federal troops will not usually use their bayonets. We often find that the demonstrators will sit or lie in front of the police. An arrest unit should then be employed to arrest the demonstrators nearest the police line.

## The Use of Water

Another degree of force is the use of water. Water is most effective on cold days and on a narrow front. It is more effective if a dye is placed in the water to aid in later identification. This will help to break up a mob as the dye will cause the individual to lose the protection that the mob gives for his actions. It should be kept in mind that water, under high pressure, can do a great deal of damage to the human body and to property.

## Selected Firing

More recent disturbances have passed from the use of a show of force to fire by selected marksman. These specially trained men must be available in the area of the disturbance to reduce indiscriminate firing. Also, a specially selected and trained marksman, armed with proper weapon, will be able to silence sniper fire more quickly, thus allowing the area to be cleared with the least amount of harm to either side.

## Full Fire Power

Finally, we must consider the most severe measure of force, full firepower. This is and must be a last resort. Every other technique must have failed. The aspects of this degree of force is all too apparent.

Again, it is to be noted that it may not be possible to employ degrees of force. Situations may develop in our republic which will require as a first step, the full firepower of the control force.

## LEGAL RESPONSIBILITIES

We turn our attention now to the aspect faced by the individual police officer and soldier, his legal responsibilities for his action in the effort to restore order.

Each state will have different laws affecting state and city forces. In some, the National Guard will have the power of arrest and in others he will not. While some states will declare a person guiltless if a rioter is killed while being arrested (88), it does not mean that if the killing was an unnecessary or malicious act, that the doer is in fact guiltless. A police officer or National Guardsman may be tried in a criminal court or a civil court for his actions. If a member of the control force internalizes and loses control of his actions, he may well suffer at a later time.

The legal standing of federal personnel is better defined than that of state military forces. First, the federal force member is responsible only to his military superiors. In no case will he take orders from the state forces. The National Guard may control active Army forces after the National Guard has been federalized. As with state forces, the member of the federal force may be held responsible for his actions in civil and criminal courts. However, the federal force member will be tried in a federal district court, which would eliminate the emotions that might be present in a state court.

---

88. Clarence M. Kelley, *Procedural Instruction #69-4 Control of Civil Disorder,* (Kansas City, 1969), p. 2.

The individual, who is a member of a control force, must direct all his efforts to the mission at hand. He must not attempt to punish and must remember that he is responsible for his actions, even when under orders. He must have patience, must be calm, must be fair, and must be firm. He must be prepared to make the mob respond and must not bluff. The officer or soldier must not take sides and must stand his ground as part of the team.

## SUMMARY

No one, for one minute, would doubt or question the ready existence of adequate means of bringing to bear on almost any situation sufficient raw power, be it by an individual patrolman with his sidearm, baton, Mace, or some other impressive device or technique, or by a riot control element with its tear gas, dogs, or water as crowd-breaking procedures. The foremost consideration must be the legal and moral aspects of the utilization of these items of equipment or methods of mission accomplishment. The use of these, even in the slightest degree beyond what is absolutely necessary in the accomplishment of their responsibilities, is inexcusable and worthy of the public's attention, criticism, and possible censure, since the establishment of existing laws, both moral and legal, was for the benefit of and compliance by all that they serve. Generally, these must include and bind to compliance *all,* not exempting any individuals or groups without adequate reason, and making those who, without just reason, violate these laws, be he criminal, citizen or law enforcement officer, a "lawbreaker."

Supreme Court Justice Louis Brandeis wrote, "Crime is contagious. If the government becomes a lawbreaker, it breeds contempt for Law. It invites every man to become a law unto himself. To declare that, in the administration of the criminal law, the end justifies the means — to declare that the government may commit crimes in order to secure the conviction of a private criminal would bring terrible retribution."

# Chapter 11

# DEMONSTRATIONS, RIOTS, AND GUERRILLA WARFARE

ONE of the fundamental rights of an American is to be able to peacefully assemble for redress of grievances. Because it is a basic right, law enforcement personnel must do everything within their power to guarantee citizens access to it. Demonstrations by lawfully orientated and dedicated individuals and groups for meaningful purposes have affected change in the past and will have future effects on our political and economic status.

## LAWFUL ASSEMBLIES

A lawful assembly of citizens is usually of little concern to the law enforcement community. Whether it is a parade or a picket line, the proper authorities have been notified of the required information and have agreed to its legality. The usual required information that is needed is — What is the nature of the assembly? Where it is to be held? Who are the people in charge of the assembly? How long will it last? And what is the composition of the group (students, union demonstrators, etc.)?

Any group that is willing to supply the needed information and is willing to obey the necessary guidelines that may have to be established already indicated that they will probably be no problem to the local police agency. Often the leaders of this type of planned assembly will confer with the authorities prior to the demonstration so that no misunderstandings will exist.

## UNLAWFUL ASSEMBLIES

An unlawful assembly or demonstration, among other things, is not usually brought to the attention of the proper civil authorities by its leaders. Another item of concern is that the individuals who are in charge of the unlawful assembly will not agree to proper controls. The reasoning is obvious – they do not intend to assemble peacefully to demonstrate in a lawful manner.

It is the responsibility of the local police agency's intelligence unit to furnish the needed information so that adequate police planning can be established. The who, what, where, when, why, and how questions must be answered prior to the demonstration. Because the intelligence unit works daily with most of the type of individuals and organizations that will be a part of an unlawful assembly, it is natural that they should be able to supply the required data.

Unlawful assemblies appear to be spontaneous situations which are the natural result of something that incurred the wrath of the people. Among other things, the most recently used reason is the arrest of an individual or a group of individuals. Many of the major demonstrations which have eventually led to riots have used this excuse for their existence. To the police agency the reason for the unlawful assembly is not as important as the immediate question of how to break up a body of protestors without having a demonstration evolve into a riot situation.

## Riots

Major portions of texts have dealt with the basic problems surrounding riot situations and how to restore order effectively. Most authorities feel that a show of force is usually required to demonstrate that police personnel are trained and ready to perform their duty. Of course the often-referred-to formations are necessary to split up the larger groups into smaller and smaller groups until the demonstrators leave the area knowing that they have been divided and have lost control.

A well-trained group of officers with the proper training in riot control, armed with the proper equipment and given proper authority to act quickly and efficiently will promptly solve the immediate situation. It is only when authorities fail to act decisively or when police officers are expected to wait for a miracle, or are sent to a riot scene with orders not to shoot, that we see problems occur. The maintenance of law and order is a law enforcement task. When politics are interjected, problems are sure to follow. If the situation becomes serious, law enforcement is usually the scapegoat. It is unfortunate that the average citizen does not realize that the police agency can only do what it is politically capable of doing. If an area is left to burn and lawful citizens are unprotected, it can usually be traced back to a political intervention into the police task.

## COLLEGE CAMPUS DEMONSTRATIONS

Throughout the history of college education there have always been forms of demonstrations initiated by students. With the "free speech" movement at the University of California campus at Berkeley, California, only a few years ago, it has become apparent that problems on college campuses were going to accelerate. In a short span of time what was feared by police officials materialized — a nationwide college revolution.

## WHO IS RESPONSIBLE?

It would be unfair to take a firm stand that all demands that have been made by various student demonstration leaders were unreasonable or unjust. In most cases, issues that would appeal to the majority of the students have been selected. The lack of adequate parking facilities, bookstore prices, and other such areas of interest have been target issues. If these issues were resolved, substitute issues not as universally accepted were used. Secondary issues might range from demanding black study courses to the hiring of a communist instructor to demonstrate "academic freedom" from politics.

Not all demonstrations on the college campuses throughout our republic have been violent confrontations. The majority have been, however, well planned and well financed. Who would help organize and finance college disorders? Every police officer who has been aware of what is going on in our country knows the answer. Without wanting to be looking under beds for Communists, it appears obvious that a good portion of our problems must be their doing. When police intelligence personnel can predict college disorders with the arrival of known agitators many who are Communist identified or self-admitted revolutionaries, some strong suspicions should arise. When literature, slogans, and songs are standardized to meet the needs of all the college demonstrations, again, a strong suspicion should arise as to who is responsible. If the standardization of tactics and so forth are not enough to create strong suspicions, perhaps, the direct tie-in of the various slogans and songs to what has been historically accepted as Communist doctrine might prove to be the final proof of who is behind the college disorders.

There is no doubt but that the youth of our country are one of the Communist priorities. Through a small dedicated group of Communist teachers a great deal has been accomplished. Their main ally has been the "liberal" colleague who is always ready to prove he is for "progress," "academic freedom," and other ideals that demonstrate that he is an intellectual. Lenin informed us of the Communist strategy many years ago when he stated: "Only by radically remolding the teaching, organization and training of the youth shall we be able to insure that the efforts of the younger generation will result in the creation of a society that will be unlike the old society, i.e. in the creation of a communist society."

Gary Allen in his article "Red Teachers" points out the dedication of the Communist college instructor:

> What Communism expects of its teachers was revealed dramatically by the late Professor Bella V. Dodd, a defected member of the National Committee of the Communist Party. In testimony before committees of both the Senate and House, and through information given to the FBI in the fifties after she left the Party, Dr. Dodd emphasized again and again: ". . . There is no such thing as freedom for a Communist college teacher. . . . The Communist teacher has a very definite function to perform. He must not only make himself an agent of the class struggle; he must indoctrinate other teachers in the class struggle, and he must see that their students are indoctrinated in the class struggle . . . the student is considered to be in rebellion against the bourgeois state. It is the function of the teacher to fan that rebellion and to make the student recognize that only by establishing a Soviet system of government will you be able to be free. . . . There is no doubt about it. This was the function of a Communist teacher: To create people who would be ready to accept the Communist regime."

## AUTHORITY TO ACT

Besides the problem of college demonstrations and riots being a united Communist target, another great difficulty for the police service is obtaining the authority to act on college campuses. An example of a common type of situation might be in order to demonstrate the extent of the problem.

A police intelligence unit has confirmed information that a known Communist campus agitator is in town. Further investigation also indicates that his target is a local college. When the president of the college is notified of the facts, he indicates that he will take care of the situation. Ill-equipped to handle what will soon become a law enforcement problem the situation usually accelerates to the point where the college officials feel the urgent need to obtain police protection.

Being a state or private institution, the police are "invited" to assist the college. Some college administrators have gone so far as to even dictate how many police officers they want and what equipment they may or may not use on the college campus.

The problem on college campuses is twofold: the inability to attempt to stop a major confrontation by controlling it at its early stages, because of the restriction of authority, and the usual dismissal of charges by the college officials after arrests have been made. Dismissing charges against a rioter is akin to giving a thief a license to steal. Policemen realize this simple fact, but some college authorities seem to forget the differences between students and criminals.

## GUERRILLA WARFARE

The term guerrilla warfare might sound out of place in a police science text; however, it should be a very definite consideration of every law enforcement officer. The purpose of this section of the text is to explore recent events and to determine if the law enforcement community is ready to accept the challenge of its adversaries.

### Administrative Attitudes

Unfortunately many police administrators have not seriously

considered the possibility of a confrontation between police personnel and determined revolutionists using guerrilla warfare techniques. The amazing thing is that the facts are not hidden but out in the open for every concerned citizen, police officer, and police administrator to take note of. One out of the hundreds of incidents reported found its way into the *Chicago Tribune,* Sunday, March 22, 1970. The bold print stated "City's Police Face Peril of Snipers Daily." Mayor Daley was quoted as saying, "if a policeman wearing a uniform and riding in a marked vehicle on patrol can be attacked, then everyone is in great jeopardy." What the mayor failed to see is that even though a sniper could shoot any citizen, the constant target is the police officer, the symbol of law and order. Since this is the case, what are police administrators doing to protect their personnel?

## Immediate Threat

Just how far along any plans might be for an extensive use of guerrilla warfare is, of course, only speculative. The threat, however, is real and is a growing concern even outside the police community. "On May 6, 1968, U.S. Representative Edwin E. Willis (then chairman of the House Committee on Un-American Activities) wrote:

> A few years ago, the overwhelming majority of Americans . . . would have scoffed at the idea of guerrilla warfare operations in the United States directed against our Government. Today, this idea does not seem as fantastic and ridiculous as it did a relatively short time ago.
>
> During the 1964 Harlem riot, Jesse Gray, the former Harlem organizer for the Communist Party, called for guerrilla warfare against the United States.
>
> This committee has received testimony indicating that agents of North Vietnam have trained some Americans in guerrilla warfare in Cuba.
>
> The Progressive Labor Party, the major Peking-orientated Communist organization in the United States . . . has distributed literature not only calling for guerrilla warfare against this country, but even spelling out how it should be conducted.
>
> Stokely Carmichael, speaking apparently for the ultramilitant black nationalist element in this country, recently stated, "Our movement is progressing toward an urban guerrilla within the United States itself."

Besides the concern of some of our high political officials who are in a position of constantly investigating and appraising threats against our government, there are other facts which should be weighed to see if there is a present threat of a large-scale guerrilla warfare action within our republic. There are of course a number of threats both verbal and printed by leaders of the "New Left" stating that the war against America will be carried out into our streets. It is apparent that some of the threats have been converted from verbal to citable instances. Are the many recent bombings and fires at our military bases coincidental or do they represent a directed effort to weaken our nation by acts of sabotage? Are large metropolitan areas becoming electrical black-out targets the actions of a few misguided individuals, or is there a reason for blackouts, i.e. to alarm the citizens and plant the seeds of fear and the general feeling that the proper authorities cannot insure the safety of the general public.

David Gumaer, in his article "Sabotage," reports:

> Headquartered in Menlo Park, California, the weird revolutionary cabal has set a target date of 1973 for a nationwide Communist takeover, preceded by assassinations and bombings. According to "inside" information revealed to Mr. Montgomery by a former Red Guard member of SDS, another leading Red Guard terrorist (an instructor at the subversive Midpeninsula Free University) has prepared an assassination list of community leaders and has revealed that "young revolutionaries, including scores of black militants, are being trained in a camp near Havana to do the job.

> Revolutionaries attending a strategy meeting in the home of the Red Guard instructor were counseled to do the following:

> Create as many police confrontations as possible. Scream "police brutality" and discredit the "pigs" to win public sympathy.

> All police and members of their families must be killed and law enforcement demoralized.

> All jails and prisons must be opened and inmates liberated.

> All counter-revolutionaries, or imperialists, who would fight "liberation" must be cut down.

> Terror is a necessary weapon and must be used to get the cooperation of the masses.

> Don't fight the draft. Go to Vietnam and shoot your commanding officer in the back.

> Become an airplane mechanic and learn to sabotage planes.

> The army can be won over from within. The police and the leaders of the establishment are our prime objectives.

The revolution has already begun, in the ghettos and in Berkeley. When the time comes weapons and explosives will be available.

## THE POLICE TARGET

The rising number of attacks on police officers may be a barometer of police frustration against symbolized authority, but what about the numerous sniper incidents directed against police personnel? Recently bombings of police equipment, police patrol units, and police stations have reached alarming proportions. Adding all of these obviously coordinated attacks on the police throughout our nation, it appears the well-known fact that law is a primary target of our revolutionaries is an undisputable conclusion.

## WHAT CAN BE DONE?

Something must be done or this impending war in our streets will become a mass massacre of the majority of our law enforcement personnel. Action must be taken now before it is completely too late. Of course the immediate danger rests in the larger cities where the great portion of hostile actions have already taken place. Secondary city police departments must also prepare to defend its citizens not only from the criminal element seeking monetary gains, but from a dedicated enemy who will fight from rooftops, sever communications, use explosives, and who will not care about what means are used to gain the objectives he is ordered to.

### All-personnel Training Concept

Even police agencies with enough personnel to create special enforcement units or riot control squads should not overlook the need to train *all* their officers in protection techniques. Now more than any other time in our history the American police officer needs more intensive training in defensive actions. No position or level should be omitted as all police officers are in jeopardy, not just the uniformed division.

In local in-service training sessions, critical city locations and targets should be emphasized, i.e. National Guard armories, and gun shops (to prevent the theft of weapons and ammunitions), communications and electrical terminals (to prevent communication destruction and blackouts), and the resident addresses of community leaders (to protect the legal authorities safety).

It has been reported that among other targets, the police faculties will be of prime concern. It is, therefore, necessary for personnel assigned to police faculties to be prepared to defend not only the total building, but especially the communications section. Needless to say, without communications the street force would become paralyzed.

## Weapons

Besides the standard weapons consisting of a 38-caliber sidearm and a police shotgun, police officers should have access to more powerful and accurate weapons. Again, as in the area of training, all officers should be able to use high-powered rifles and automatic weapons. Not only must all the men know how to use the weapons, they must also know where the weapons are stored and how to effectively distribute them.

All the weapons in the world will not benefit a police agency unless the personnel have the power to use them. A police department which openly advocates a no-shoot policy openly advertises its inadequacy. There must be an ability to use deadly force, and this decision must rest with the individual police officer. Those cities which are controlled by liberal anti-police officials who coddle the criminal elements are the first to be tested.

## Tactical Squads

Since it is apparent that the future holds greater danger for police officers, many cities have already created tactical squads or anti-sniper units. It is reasonable to assume that if nothing else, the police should be able to defend themselves in a fashion promoting the least amount of danger. The best defense against a sniper is to use similar tactics.

Members of a police tactical squad should be assigned to all shifts to maintain equal protection throughout the entire twenty-four hour period of the day. They also should have their specialized weapons readily accessible to them. A common practice by police administrators is to visibly distinguish the members of specialized units. Members of a tactical unit should not be easily identifiable. By appearing like any other officer and using regular police cruisers, no one outside of the police agency will be able to tell who and how many make up the police defense team.

## Intelligence Information

With the advent of more and more attacks on police personnel, accurate police intelligence information is becoming more critical. Greater expenditures and manpower will have to be shifted into this vital police function in order to better prepare police administration with the needed data. A greater mutual assistance between police agencies must be created so that neighborhood agencies can benefit from the knowledge gained from each department. Because of the intrusion of many anti-police orientated individuals into the law enforcement community, a sweep of investigations must be made to ascertain that all police personnel in vital positions can be trusted as part of a team to combat the revolutionary movement.

Police personnel whose interests do not lie in the direction of an effective police service must be removed. Those politicians whose past history demonstrates that they are anti-police in attitude and would further handicap law enforcement must not only be identified but also removed from the political scene if the law enforcement community is to function properly.

# Chapter 12

# ANTI-POLICE ORGANIZATIONS
## INTRODUCTION AND STATEMENT OF THE PROBLEM

COMMUNISM is the major menace of our time. There are more Communists in New York City than in Moscow. America is marked for Communism, whether it is disguised as Socialism, Progressivism, or Modernism. Never has America been in greater danger. *Never!* Of the approximately 200 million or so adult Americans now living in the United States, approximately 500,000 have at one time or another belonged to the Communist Party. We must determine how many of these "ex-Communists" have really severed their ties with Communism and how many have actually gone underground. There are pseudo ex-Communists in high places; the threat to policemen and their families is evident. Students for a Democratic Society (SDS) leader, Mike Klanshy, stated "that your home is not safe if you think you have something to protect in society."

The left wing militants believe that police prefer violence to non-violence and chaos to order. By portraying the police as their enemy and repeatedly crying police brutality they have been successful in gaining a great deal of support. It has become necessary for the militants to escalate their violence so as to continue to receive recognition to his protest. *Ramparts* magazine offered a ten thousand dollar reward to the first person providing information leading to the arrest and conviction of a police officer for first degree murder of a black person or persons. The Black Panthers have called for the killing of a cop a day.

The Communists mean what they say, "Americans are so smug and confident of their military and economic superiority that they refuse to believe that the Communists are threats." The Communist Party in America has been ordered to concentrate its efforts on youth. Activism is spreading and reaching down to the seventh grade in some communities. The United States Commissioner of Education issued a warning to high school principals and state education leaders to be on their guard: "The number of incidents is likely to increase this year as students join in the general activism." Marxist-Leninist dogma has always proclaimed that to win the youth for Communism is to win the future. Lenin proclaimed, "Give us the child for eight years and it will be a Bolshevik forever." It is only when youth movements have launched a total attack against democratic societies that destruction of that society has been achieved. Revolution comes from the youth, not from the ranks of the senior citizens. Russia may not be providing outright support to the youth movement in America but she is certainly applauding it. One of the most sinister youth movements of the late twenties was the Rumanian terrorist band, the Archangel Michael, which later became the Iron Guard. Members of the Fascist youth movements were mainly sadistic, blindly destructive young thugs who preached a doctrine of violence. The most significant aspect of youth movements is that they have never been willing to accept the lessons of the past.

Democracy has always been seen as an irretrievable part of the whole rotten system and all politicians have been seen as crooks. Equally common to all youth groups is a profound pessimism about the future of present-day culture. Present militant youth movements are little different from most youth movements in the last hundred years which have had definite political aims and found common ground in Bolshevik movements. Youth movements have always been extremely emotional. Underlying their beliefs has always been a common anti-capitalist, anti-bourgeois denominator, a conviction that the established order is corrupt to the bones and beyond redemption by parliamentary means of reform.

The two major militant groups of the New Left are the Black Panthers and the SDS, each of which has several other front groups and similarly affiliated organizations. Both the Black Panthers and the SDS conform to the classic image of the Communist militant. Some of the same international links which unite the supporters of the Viet Cong also serve to unite the leftist organizers of student protests and black power. Most prominent in major campus disorders today is the SDS. A good many disorders have been instigated by other groups, such as the Black Student

Union (BSU), but SDS soon joins in and takes over.

Communist activities afford a form of release to those who feel a sense of insecurity or inadequacy in their personal lives. It provides a retreat for those who cannot bear the responsibility of individual decision or action. Conversely, those possessed by the will for power to dominate and exert authority over others find Communism satisfying. With fewer than fifty members the SDS has been able to seize campus issues and obtain a great deal of support and create a disruptive influence. SDS leaders favor violent revolution. The SDS and Black Panthers are using the civil rights in their hopeful attempt to destroy this country and capitalism.

SDS is the armed warrior of anti-education. It makes no secret of its desire to destroy American Democratic Society and the universities, which it considers a faithful replica of that iniquitous society. Communists object to investigations as a threat to their "human rights" or "civil rights." Americans should realize this. Former Senator Bill Jenner of Indiana stated, "A rat hunt is not a witch hunt."

The militant student left includes SDS, New Leftists, left Liberals, old leftists, frauds, hippies, social democrats, libertarians, pacifists, humanitarians, anarchists, opportunists, idealists, and adventurers. The black militants include self-styled Troskyites, Maoists, anarchists, nihilists, and Black Power advocates all mixed in an attempt to undermine discipline and morale. Despite the bewildering variety of "front" names employed a number of individuals in these groups have been traced back to old line pro-Communist organizations, which are now split to some extent into pro-Russian and pro-Maoist camps.

There is little "new" about the New Left. Too often, effects of typical Communist Party cliches and techniques are apparent. The slogan "Student Power" made its first appearance at the *Goettingen Studententag* in 1920. Class against class, a term was introduced by the Communists, and the chasm created between the people made it possible for Hitler to take power. The Black Panther "Free Huey" campaign is not unlike the Communist Party drive through such fronts as the Citizens Committee to Free Earl Browder, which was successful in getting President Roosevelt to commute the sentence of and to free Earl Browder, a Communist convicted of passport violations in the fall of 1940. The Communists contended that Browder was a political prisoner and that release was a necessary gesture for national unity (Russia was then our ally).

The Communist Party discovered the Negroes of the South as part of their policy of "the United Front from Below." A permanent target of Communism has been the Negro community. It is a basic tenet of Leninism that an underdeveloped minority group is ripe for revolution. All that is thought necessary to bring such a group into the Communist camp is to provide it with "vanguard" leadership and a "correct" interpretation of its problems.

From the early 1920's to the present, the Communist effort to win over the Negroes as a mass has been unceasing. No tactic or stratagem has been neglected and both agitation and propaganda have been constant. The sociological attraction of Communism is based on exploitation of social injustices and inequalities. To Communists, everyone who has been the victim of some form of social injustice or prejudice is a potential recruit for Communism.

The protests of the liberal dove press of today are not unlike those of Louis Budenz, editor of the *Daily Worker* in 1941, who wrote that "The workers everywhere do not want their sons to die, mangled scraps of flesh — in order to enrich Wall Street. America keep out of this war."

We know from our intelligence sources that some of the leadership of the peace movement do not have the best interests of this country in mind. We know that plans for the demonstrations have been discussed in countries outside of the United States. Certain journalistic liberals and intellectual snobs are subverting some segment of the free press to the cause of Communism and their ultimate destruction with dismaying zeal. Snobbism and elitism of the intelligentsia have placed liberalism in a political crisis. It has blamed rioting and crime in the Negro community on the police, using them as symbols of white racism.

Militancy is increasing. Some signs on Chicago's West Side are, "Your God better have a rod. Mine does." with a picture of a black man holding a rifle; "He came down into the valley so he could keep saying – I am a revolutionary." with a picture of Illinois Black Panther Fred Hampton; "Don't Vote – All power to the people – Black Power to Black People." These people mean to loot, burn, and kill. They are after our country and mean to destroy everything in which we believe. Never before in the history of the United States have policemen been faced with graver danger or a more serious threat than posed by the Communist revolutionaries presently wagering war against them and our society which they are defending. Robert W. Finn, Detective Inspector, Minneapolis Police Department stated, "Now that we have guerrilla or commando tactics, rioters have found out that they cannot win in a major confrontation with police – these smaller operations are harder to control." Dissension and public disorder arising out of induced racial conflicts are already creating some paralysis within municipal police. Dr. Douglas Knight, who resigned as President of Duke University stated for his reason, "To protect my family." Policemen in many cities are reacting similarly as they see a distinct threat to the safety of their families. Dr. Allan P. Sindler resigned as Chairman of the Department of Government, Cornell University stating, "We no longer can teach in the way we wish to teach them. Students insist we tell them what they want to hear rather than what we believe to be true." By admitting substandard students under EOP, colleges have brought most of the trouble upon themselves.

Arson tactics are being used more this year by militants both black and white. Guerrilla tactics aimed at rendering the institutions, schools, police, etc. inoperable, are escalating. The Communist militants are using ambush tactics in their war against police. The growing tactic this year will be guerrilla warfare. Blacks and whites are arming in large numbers in fear of racial eruption. A pattern shared by the rest of the country is expressed by an Orange County, Calfornia car dealer, "There are very few colored in Orange County, but in case of rioting, I'd use my gun for self-preservation. Most people would protect their property same as I would. Ninety-five percent of my friends would do the same thing, and they almost all have guns." Some predict an open civil war with house to house street fighting resulting from the fear generated by this attack against our thin blue line of defense.

American people by the millions are unwittingly aiding the Communists thus cooperating in their own destruction. For every trained, hardcore Communist, there are at least ten other persons under Communist discipline who contribute to political subversion, espionage, and potential sabotage. Further, for each of these ten there are at least ten more Communist dupes working just as strongly for them unknowingly thus, figured on a base of 50,000 card carrying members, they have at least 5,000,000 people on their side in the United States. This is 2.5 percent of our population, which is quite a sizable portion when one considers that only about 3.5 percent at the most took part in the French Revolution. It is always a small minority which carries out a successful revolution, no matter if it is for a just or unjust cause.

Communism must be stopped, it must be fought, or America is lost. Americans must rededicate themselves to the American way of life and uphold the concepts of basic constitutional government, oppose the persecution of patriots, demand American conduct by elected representatives, and rid the nation of its infestation of Communists, pro-Communists, fellow-travelers, progressives, socialists, modernists, etc., who are directing America toward destruction.

## YOUTH MOVEMENTS

Revolutions have always been youth movements, and usually the militant leaders have been the young. Youth are not yet integrated into society and are unencumbered by the ties of family or professional careers. Young people are freer than other elements of society. It has been shown throughout history that student revolution is by far not a new idea. History is indeed repeating herself.

At universities of the Middle Ages, the police were openly ridiculed by students. The universities did nothing to exact discipline from their own scholars. Students' morals were appalling, and their comings and goings were considered a private affair. The University was a great concourse of men and boys freed from all parental restriction. It was a place characterized by bloody affrays, pitched battles, mayhem, rape, and homicide.

From time to time, the citizenry would get even by killing a few students. In 1354, the real troublemakers were a minority; some of them were not even students but young vagabonds enjoying the immunities of the scholar, drifting from university to university.

Only in later ages did the university begin to impose stricter disciplinary actions on students. As a rule, youth movements prosper only against a background of rising affluence. Karl Marx rebelled not only against Christianity which his parents had embraced but also against capitalism which had made his father a wealthy man and had given Marx every opportunity that wealth affords. This parodox is typical of the revolting youth movements and is as true today. The German Neue Schar of 1919 were the original hippies – long-haired, sandaled, they castigated urban civilization, read Hermann Hesse and Indian philosophy, practiced free love, and distributed flowers in their meetings. They danced and sang to the music of the guitar and attended lectures on the "revolution of the soul." The German youth movement began as an unpolitical form of opposition to a civilization that had little to offer the young generation, a protest against the lack of vitality, warmth, emotion, and ideals in German society. It wanted to develop qualities of sincerity, decency, openmindedness, to free its members from petty egoism and careerism, to oppose artificial conventions, snobbery, and affectation. This movement was of course exploited, and the unpoliticalness of it ended with the first world war. It was easily swayed in different directions by philosophical charlatans and political demagogues preaching all kinds of eccentric doctrines.

By 1930 the youth movement was displaying an incontinent eagerness to rid Germany of democracy. Lacking experience and imagination, they clearly misjudged the major political forces of their time. The Nazi student movement called on students to join the ranks of the workers. The fascist experience has shown that the immense potential which is inherent in every youth movement can be exploited in the most disastrous way. (America lies in a state of grave danger. We must channel this immense potential in the right direction, cultivate it, and lead it to help build, not destroy, America.) The American youth movement with its immense idealistic potential has gone badly, perhaps irrevocably, off the rails.

Communists try to exploit student dissent and marshal it against free-world government and institutions. To students who transform themselves in imagination into members of the revolutionary "new proletariat" it offers the romantic satisfaction of joining a struggle against an abstraction which is scarcely intelligible, alienation, and toward an objective which is barely conceivable, let alone achievable, a socialist anarchist utopia.

Party membership gives one the feeling of being part of a disciplined and organized group which knows where it is going and satisfaction in working in the interests of "humanity." Party members hold a self-conceived conception of being an enlightened segment of society, the "vanguard" of the working class, an elite leadership group, the "wave" of the future.

Various other reasons why people participate in Communist activities are the temporary thrill of secretive work, personal weaknesses, blackmail, feelings of spite against America, or because of an imagined wrong. Very important is ideological motivation, an attraction to the theory of Communism and/or misguided admiration for Soviet rule in Russia. Many persons harbor latent Communist tendencies which a skillful Communist agitator can bring to the surface by appealing to their emotions.

Only the person who himself hates is likely to become a willing and skillful fomenter of hatred, able to stir up and exploit animosities wherever the Party, for tactical reasons, wants them to exist. In 1920, Lenin stated that wherever mutual animosities and rivalries exist between non-Communist groups and nations, the Party's practical task is to take advantage of this hostility and to incite one against the other. The Communists have been following this tactic ever since − setting nation against nation, employee against employer, race against race. It takes experienced haters, with no qualms, to apply a method of this sort.

The revolt of American college students in the 1960's is now entering an accelerated stage. It began at the University of California at Berkeley in the autumn of 1964 and is reaching unprecedented proportions. Leaders, often not college students, use the schools as a base for carrying antiwar campaigns to surrounding communities. At Berkeley there is an open split between radicalism with a rational analysis and program and "militancy" empty of political content. SDS leader, Mike Klansky, has criticized the American system as "racist, capitalist, and imperialist." He has advocated stodent radicals' arming themselves. SDS leaders have rejected the possibility of change coming from within American society and turned romantically to HO, Che, and the peasant masses of the Third World.

### The Students for a Democratic Society

SDS not only poses a serious ideological and militant threat, especially with the Maoism, but a moral threat by sociopaths like those who form the most militant faction; this group has eliminated whatever political content might originally exist in the New Left by denying the possibility of individual sanity in a corrupt society and resorting to mental terrorism.

The wave of student disorders has brought personal injury, death, and millions of dollars worth of property damage and has disrupted the education of many earnest students. The student revolt is shifting from massive confrontations to guerrilla warfare with hit-and-run tactics being employed.

In late March of 1969, the SDS held a national council meeting in Austin, Texas. Following that meeting the tempo of campus disorders has substantially increased. Examples are as follows:

1. Harvard, April 9, SDS led students forcibly ejected officials from administration building.

2. American University, April 23, SDS occupied administration building.

3. George Washington University, April 24, SDS occupied the Institute for Sino-Soviet Studies.

4. University of Washington, April 24, SDS demonstration succeeded in halting the operation of the student placement center.

5. Columbia University, April 30, SDS took over two university buildings.

6. Stanford University, SDS occupied Administration Building.

7. Northeastern University, May 13, SDS led students took over a meeting room and lounge.

Although there are some differences between the Black Panther and SDS, their similarities are most important. Both advocate the violent overthrow of our government and are Communist inspired. Both have high regard for Mao's little red book and guerrilla warfare tactics. Reasons for membership in both groups is quite the same and is similar to the attraction found by members of all Communist groups which have existed.

It is interesting to note that the FBI 1969 Annual Report stated that in 1969 major disorders erupted on some 225 campuses, causing three million dollars in property damage and resulted in over four thousand arrests. The majority of these disorders can be directly or indirectly credited to the SDS. The SDS is by no means a small problem. Their membership has been estimated at 40,000, and there are some 250 chapters in existence.

### The Black Panther Party

The Black Panther Party, a virulent self-styled armed revolutionary vanguard, was organized in 1966 principally by twenty-five-year-old Huey Newton and thirty-year-old Bobby Seal. The significance of the name Black Panther was borrowed from the Lowndes County Freedom Organization in Alabama.

The Black Panthers are the largest and fastest growing of the ultraradical groups currently organized in the Negro community. In less than two years, the Panthers have mushroomed from a 125 man contigent based solely in Oakland, California, to a nationwide operation with sixty thousand sympathizers and established chapters in two dozen cities. Each chapter is organized into small units in the various communities throughout the cities. Each unit has a captain; these captains along with Newton and Seal and a treasurer made up an executive committee which set the basic policy for the entire organization.

Schooled in the Marxist-Leninist idealogy and the teachings of Mao Tse-tung, the Panthers have updated their theology by adding the teachings of Marcus Garvey, W.E.B. DuBois, and Malcolm X., black men who have each been significant in the "struggle of black people." These men are some of the Panthers' heroes, and their writings are required reading for young Black Panthers in training.

The dollars that fuel the Black Panther Party come from a variety of domestic sources both legal and illegal. The largest source of Panther funds is not the poverty program, however, but the armed robberies and the shakedowns committed in the name of revolution. The Panther's "Breakfast Program" is a perfect example. Tough young recruits swagger through the ghetto informing merchants that the Panthers are running preschool food lines for underprivileged black children. Contributions in the form of foodstuffs or money are demanded. "You wouldn't want someone to burn down your store," smiled one Los Angeles Panther.

The merchants soon get the message. In the San Francisco area, an auto dealer refused to give the Panthers money. When he arrived at his place of business the next day, he found his plate-glass windows shattered.

Like most revolutionaries, the leaders of the Black Panther Party do not come from the bottom of the economic ladder. Huey Newton could have escaped from the ghetto if he had wanted to. He went to the integrated and excellent Berkeley High School and eventually spent a year in law school. Bright but rebellious, he had numerous run-ins with the authorities in high school before he finally was graduated, to go on to Merritt College, a small, rundown two-year institution on the fringes of the Oakland ghetto. That was in the early nineteen sixties, when Merritt became a kind of incubator of Negro nationalism.

Both Newton and Seal, who also attended Merritt, remember the time as an exciting period of self-discovery for scores of young Oakland Blacks. They would cut classes and sit around the nearby coffee shops, arguing about the black revolution, and reading the classics of black nationalism together.

After Newton and Seal left Merritt, there was a period of political uncertainty. There was also a period of "hustling" on the "streets" for Newton and frequent arrests for theft and burglary. Eventually came a year in the county jail on an assault with a deadly weapon conviction. Newton also led riots and strikes in prison for which he was placed in solitary confinement. However, Newton took this as a challenge and attempted to always be doing push-ups whenever a guard would enter.

For Newton, as for Malcolm X, the prison experience only confirmed his hostility to the white world and made him more militant. Once outside of prison, Newton and Seal reestablished their association and began to talk about the need for a revolutionary party that would represent the black masses and the ghetto youth which to that time had never been truly represented by any civil rights group.

"We began to understand the unwritten law of force," says Bobby Seal. "They (the policy) have guns, and what the law actually says ain't worth a damn. We started to think of a program that defines and offsets this physical fact of the ghetto and came up with the Black Panther Party."

Above all, you should understand this man Eldridge Cleaver, whose recorded crime was assault but whose sin was the calculated soul-purging rape of white women. Cleaver matured from petty ghetto marijuana hustler and self-confessed rapist to the leading intellect of black liberation. As minister of information and the Panther Party's intellectual leader, he was a radical candidate for Presidency of the United States of America, adopted by the primarily white Peace and Freedom Party.

"We shall have our manhood," writes Cleaver in his extraordinary book *Soul on Ice,* written in prison. "We shall have it or the earth will be leveled by our attempts to gain it."

You should understand this man Cleaver, this Black Panther, this propagandist of the New Left, because he means exactly what he says about leveling the earth, and us with it if white society does not soon change itself radically.

The Black Panther Party has grown in direct proportion to the amount of police reaction against it. It was a tiny and relatively insignificant handful when its members marched into the California State Legislature on May 2, 1967, bearing loaded guns (then a perfectly legal act) in opposition to gun control legislation.

They have grown somewhat by the time Newton was wounded and arrested following a shoot-out with the police in which a white Oakland policeman, John Frey, died, and his partner was wounded. After that, police harassment of the Panthers intensified and so did the Party's recruitment. Before and during a widely publicised trial in which Newton was found guilty, Panther units formed in more than a dozen cities. As a result of declared irregularities in the trial, the Party has declared him to be a political prisoner of war even though he has been released on bail. He has become the hero of the Panther theme of injustice.

Bobby Seale, Chairman of the Party, an outspoken advocate of the use of force to obtain freedom, recently went to trial in Chicago along with seven white leftist activists. Seale's disruptions in the courtroom resulted first in threats of contempt by the judge who finally directed that Seale be bound and gagged. Seale continued to disrupt the procedure of the court room charging that he had been denied the right of council of his choice. The judge finally declared a mistrial in Seale's case and sentenced him on a finding of contempt of court.

Eldridge Cleaver writes from exile. He is international editor of *Ramparts* magazine, a position to which he was appointed after he fled this country to avoid being returned to jail for violating his parole. He is believed to be living in Algeria with his wife Cathline and their son.

The intensity of the attack on the Black Panther Party and its personnel is unprecedented. This is the result of the vigor with which the Panthers have attacked the power structure and its front line of defense, the police. It is not reform they are after but "the destruction of your stinking, rotton society — and you had better learn that fast."

In August, 1967, Oakland's chief of police, Robert Preston, thought the Panthers unworthy of comment. "It's not the police but society that should be concerned with groups such as this. They have on occasion harassed police and made some efforts to stir up animosity against us, but they are not deserving of any special treatment. They have made pretty ridiculous assertions which don't deserve to be dignified by anyone commenting on them." If Chief Preston were to comment on the role of the Black Panthers today, he would admit that he has taken "special" steps to cope with the threat of this radical group to the welfare of his men.

"We are organized like guerrillas," said minister of education, George Mason Murray, while visiting Cuba in August 1968; "our purpose: to assassinate police, blow up bridges, burn factories."

This is not idle rhetoric; detailed instruction on the revolutionary use of explosives was revealed in Senate testimony last year. Donald Lee Cox held classes in Alabama for young Negroes in the manufacture and use of acid bombs, resulting in a wave of terrorist bombings, mostly of Mobile business establishments. At least fifty-eight of the bombings were attributed to such explosives.

The Panthers have been criticized for their provocative actions by other black militants. Said one such militant, "These cats have just been playing cowboys and Indians." To write off the Panthers as a fringe group is to miss the point altogether. It is more important to face the fact that their existence is only the reflection of a much deeper problem which has gone unattended much too long, that of racism.

The Kerner Commission Report, while suggesting many cures to curb riots, such as developing greater rapport between police and the ghettos, attributed the basic cause of black resentment to white racism. Nicholas Katzenbach, formerly with the Justice Department, put it this way: "In many places, we have law and order without justice, operating extraconstitutionally. Often it is really nothing more than socially condoned violence." It is doubtful that the majority will agree with a point of view that is self-indicting: "We have met the enemy and he is us."

WHAT WE WANT: WHAT WE BELIEVE – The Panther Philosophy

We believe we can end police brutality in our black community by organizing black self-defense groups that are dedicated to defending our black community from racist police oppression and brutality. The Second Amendment to the Constitution of the United States gives a right to bear arms. We therefore believe that all black people should arm themselves for self-defense.

We want all black people when brought to trial to be tried in court by a jury of their peer group or people from their own black community, as defined by the Constitution. We believe that the courts should follow the United States Constitution so that black people will receive fair trials. A peer is a person from a similar economic, social, religious, geographical, environmental, historical, and racial background. To do this the court will be forced to select a jury from the black community from which the black defendant came. We have been and are being tried by all-white juries that have no understanding of the "average reasoning man" of the black community.

We want full employment for our people. We believe that the federal government is responsible and obligated to give every man employment or a guaranteed income. We believe that if the white American businessmen will not give full employment, then the means of production should be taken from the businessman and placed in the hands of the community so that the people of the community can organize and employ all of its people and give a high standard of living.

We believe that this racist capitalistic government has robbed us and now we are demanding the overdue payment of forty acres of land and two mules. Forty acres and two mules was promised one hundred years ago as restitution for slave labor and mass murder of black people. The American racist has taken part in the slaughter of over fifty million black people. The Germans are now aiding the Jews in Israel for the genocide of the Jewish people; therefore, we feel that ours is a modest demand.

## How the Revolution Will Succeed

Blacks in cities across the nation have learned from Watts a means of resistance fighting by amassing the people in the streets, throwing bricks and Molotov cocktails to destroy property and create disruption. But when the people are massed in the streets, they can be easily herded into a small area by the police and shortly contained often by brutal violence. This manner of resistance is sporadic, short-lived, and costly in violence against the people. In a riot situation, the first man who throws a Molotov cocktail may not be known personally by the masses, but yet his action is respected in accordance with prevailing standards and as such is followed by the people. This incorrect tactic of resistance fighting has been transmitted to the ghettos of the Black nation across the country.

The Black Panther Party must provide leadership for the people. It must teach the correct strategic methods of prolonged resistance through literature and activities. If the activities of the party are respected by the people, the people will follow the example. This is the primary job of the party. As the people learn that it is no longer advantageous for them to resist by going into the streets in large numbers, and when they see the advantages of guerrilla tactics, they will quickly adopt it.

Blacks in this country are cast in a role as "colonial" people, and as such are at war with their conquerors; the police are an army of occupation, deployed to keep down insurrection. Black men in jail are prisoners of war; the major communications media are propaganda instruments of the white colonialists. Only viewed in this context can this new left movement in black America be viewed. This movement is different from all forerunning black rights movements in that it is not limiting itself to blacks and is not geared to reform. Its goal is revolution. Capitalism must be replaced with a people's form of socialism in which the economy is geared to meet the needs of the people rather than to produce raw profit.

The Black Panther Party, as the vanguard of the people's revolution, cannot tolerate racism. In the spirit of revolution, we must put away petty "hangups" of racial prejudice and get on with the business at hand. "Black power to black people; white power to white people; all power to all the people." As right thinking men of good will see the fallacy of this system of government which is built on deprivation of the poor to sustain the wealthy, they will renounce the system and cast their lot with the poor people of the earth.

## THE AMERICAN CIVIL LIBERTIES UNION

In the preceding pages obvious anti-police organizations were discussed. Any person who spends only a small amount of time exploring the tenets of Communism, the SDS, and the Black Panther Party, will soon come to the conclusion that these organizations are definitely in conflict with the law enforcement community as well as with the American public in general. Anti-police organizations are just that — groups of individuals who consider the police their enemy and will do whatever they can to render law enforcement ineffective. Some of the more radical individuals and groups are dedicated to assassinate any representative of the law.

Let us now turn our attention to groups and individuals who do not openly defy the law or let themselves become the leaders of a revolution, but do the tasks or secondary functions to assist the goals of the Communists. Of course the first organization that comes to the mind of knowledgeable law enforcement personnel is the American Civil Liberties Union (ACLU).

Before we explore the history and goals of this organization, it might be well to note that a so-called police authority only a short time ago advocated that law enforcement personnel join this organization. In a current text this man also indicates that for a police officer to look upon the ACLU with suspicion is a symptom of a paranoid tendency. For any officer of the law to neglect investigation and look upon the ACLU with anything less than suspicion would be a dereliction of duty. No man or group of men will ever sway the opinion of the bulk of police personnel to see the ACLU in a favorable position when the facts are so clear for all to see.

David Emerson Gumaer wrote an article entitled "The ACLU" for *the American Opinion* in September, 1969. The article is well documented and is an excellent source of information on just who the ACLU is and what it stands for. One of the interesting areas that Mr. Gumaer delves into is the alarming number of known, identified, or self-admitted Communists who have been not only members, but officers of this organization. A common remark by many of the "Liberals" when this fact is mentioned is that just because there are a number of Communists in the ACLU does not make the organization Communist. They insist that there are many good Americans who also hold membership. An easy reply to this type of thinking is a well-known fact to policemen: A "good" boy does not associate with delinquents. A "good" citizen does not associate with criminals. It may be unfair to judge one by the company he keeps, but it is usually an accurate indication.

## History of the ACLU

The history of the ACLU is marked with the warnings of various legislative committees that the organization is established to aid the Communists and therefore an enemy of the American way of life. One fact to note however, is that the ACLU has never been designated as a Communist Front Organization by the United States Attorney General.

As far back as January 17, 1931, we find the Fish Committee

Report concluding its investigation with this strong statement:

> The American Civil Liberties Union is closely affiliated with the Communist movement in the United States, and fully ninety percent of its efforts are on behalf of Communists who have come into conflict with the law. It claims to stand for free speech, free press, and free assembly; but it is quite apparent that the main function of the A.C.L.U. is to attempt to protect the Communists in their advocacy of force and violence to overthrow the government, replacing the American flag by the Red flag and erecting a Soviet Government in the place of the republican form of government guaranteed to each State by the Federal Constitution.

This House Committee further concurred with an exhaustive Report issued by the Lusk Committee of the New York State Legislature, in both 1920 and 1928. That Committee has decided (after hearing Roger Baldwin's testimony) that:

> The American Civil Liberties Union, in the last analysis, is a supporter of all subversive movements; its propaganda is detrimental to the interests of the State. It attempts not only to protect crime but to encourage attacks upon our institutions in every form.

In 1966 the National Conference of Police Associations report of the Counter-Subversive Committee stated in part: "In our opinion, the ACLU and its brother organizations have mastered the technique of Joseph Goebbels and practiced by Moscow Communists to the nth degree." There are many other reports and comments by *proven* authorities in the law enforcement field that the ACLU is a cancer to the police service. For anyone to indicate or openly state that the ACLU is anything less than an enemy of the law enforcement community is an indictment of ignorance.

## Legal Assistance

Many people are fooled by the name American Civil Liberties Union connoting defenders of civil liberties. We must ask, whose civil liberties? All Americans equally, or whom? Of course the advocated objective of the ACLU is to render legal assistance to those who need it. Unfortunately those who require the assistance of the ACLU usually turn out to be in a position adverse to the legally constituted law. Perhaps not all of the individuals and groups who have been assisted have been revolutionaries, but the emphasis appears to be in protecting left wing radicals and known Communists.

Has the ACLU been successful in its many attempts to aid the enemy? When in American history has the country allowed identified adverse agents to hold security positions? We do now, for a Communist cannot be denied employment in our defense industry on the reasoning that he is a dedicated enemy of the country. This is a clear victory over our country's security for the Communist Party.

The fight to oppose loyalty oaths in our schools, defense plants, and governmental positions has been taken to the Supreme Court by those friends of civil liberties, the ACLU. Naturally loyalty oaths and the registration of Communists are of paramount concern to these "loyal Americans." Of course any person wishing to charge police personnel with the common complaints of police brutality will find a ready legal assistance with his local office of the ACLU.

## A POLICE RESPONSIBILITY

It is a police officer's responsibility to know his enemies and what they stand for. It is time for the police service to start to take the offensive against the smug Liberal and his close associate, the Communist. The American people are beginning to ask questions as to what is wrong in our country. Many of our citizens who just did not care or did not have time to become involved a short time ago are beginning to become concerned. Let us not have this rebirth of patriotism go unnoticed. With the proper education of who are the enemies of the nation and what can be done to help our country get back on its feet, obvious future defeat can be turned into victory. Those organizations who are the backbone and the workhorse of the Communist conspiracy must be exposed. Obvious subversive information within the law enforcement community must be *in some cases* made public knowledge.

# Chapter 13

# POLICE ORGANIZATIONS

## INTRODUCTION

THE purpose of this chapter is to provide information on national police organizations and their contributions to the police service. There are almost 500,000 police officers who are directly involved in law enforcement in one way or another. There are approximately 40,000 separate law enforcement agencies with a total annual budget of three billion dollars. This amount includes all federal, state, county, and municipal police agencies.

It is realized that there are many outstanding local, county, and state police organizations which have contributed and will continue to contribute a great deal towards the efforts of effective law enforcement. Most of these local organizations are geared to the needs of the local law enforcement officers. There can be no dispute to the fact that the greatest advances by local police agencies have been through the efforts of their own police fraternities, associations, and chapters. The advancement on the national level, however, will always come from the efforts of the many outstanding national police associations. One of the major benefits derived from membership in a national police association is that it is through national associations that we find the greatest efforts to unite the police personnel and to advance a form of professionalism. Many national police associations are established to assist the law enforcement community with many of the various problems already discussed in this text.

## THE NATIONAL POLICE OFFICERS'
## ASSOCIATION OF AMERICA

The National Police Officers' Association of America is a nonprofit organization of law enforcement officers of all ranks and agencies throughout our nation. It was established for the purpose of recognizing acts of valor and sacrifices made by law enforcement officers. It also maintains the only National Police Hall of Fame Memorial, which is dedicated to those police officers killed in the line of duty. The NPOAA is a strong supporter of an enforceable code of ethics for law enforcement. It attempts to achieve a better understanding between the police and the average American citizen, and it is a dedicated adversary of those who would attempt to create a police civilian review board. The basic requirement for membership in the NPOAA is that the applicant be a full-time law enforcement officer of either a federal, state, county, or local police agency. The benefits of membership in this very worthy police association are many. There is a $5,000 life insurance policy for all full-time members. False arrest insurance is also available at a minimum cost. The National Police Academy offers many fine correspondence courses including Marksmanship, Criminal Investigation, Traffic Accident Investigation, Police Operational Intelligence, Confessions and Statements, and Police Community Relations. Many other areas of police science courses will also soon be added to give the academy a complete scope of all the vital law enforcement subjects.

The association also publishes its magazine, *VALOR,* the official police review. The magazine is published quarterly and is sent to all members. *VALOR* not only prints articles which are of interest and importance to all police personnel but also has a section which deals with all the latest legislative and judicial changes throughout our country. The NPOAA is unique as a national police organization in that it has become the national voice for police officers. *VALOR* has taken that extra step in that it attempts to enlighten its members of not only police but political matters which affect the police community.

Membership in the National Police Officers' Association of America is obtained through application to its headquarters at 1890 South Tamiami Trail, Venice, Florida. The cost of membership is ten dollars a year.

## THE NATIONAL POLICE RESERVE OFFICERS ASSOCIATION

The NPROA was formed to give opportunity to those

individuals who are not in actual law enforcement work, but who are interested in law enforcement, to become part of a police reserves association. Membership is open to all security personnel, industrial or private, police reserve officers, and law enforcement college students and instructors. The basic idea of the NPROA is to bridge the gap between law enforcement and those individuals who are interested in police service. Reserve officers and other members receive *VALOR* as do the regular members of the NPOAA. Many of the other benefits of membership in the NPOAA are also available to the members of the reserve association.

Some of the activities of the NPOAA are to strive for professionalism of reserve officers and security personnel, to better prepare those students and reserve officers who wish to eventually become full-time law enforcement officers, and to assist the law enforcement community in defeating the creation of police civilian review boards.

## THE FRATERNAL ORDER OF POLICE

In 1915 a small group of policemen formed the Fraternal Order of Police to correct the injustices occurring within the police profession at that time: twelve-hour work days, seven-day work weeks, overtime without pay and depressed economic and social status. The FOP was and is to the policeman what the labor organization was to the industrial worker. There were, of course, two exceptions: the FOP enrolled everyone from patrolman to chief, and the strike was forbidden. The first lodge was formed in Pittsburgh, Pennsylvania (Ft. Pitt, Lodge No. 1).

The goals of the organization are to bind together every police officer of the country in fraternity and friendship, to defend themselves and their interests when attacked, and to gain all the rights to which they are entitled as members of the police service.

Composition of the national organization is as follows:

1. Grand lodge — Delegates from all subordinate lodges assembled in the biennial conference; board of directors manages organization between conferences. Located in Cleveland, Ohio.

2. State lodge — Made up when three or more lodges form

within a state.

3. Subordinate lodge – Formed at the request of ten or more members of a law enforcement agency.

The FOP is currently involved in attacking problems existing in police income, law enforcement education, both of the community and the policeman, and community safety.

The FOP sponsors and encourages observation of the annual "Peace Officers' Memorial Day," which is during the week in which May 15th occurs each year.

There are two kinds of membership in the FOP – active and honorary. Active membership is limited to those doing active police work full-time. Only active members have the right to vote. Officers are elected from the active membership. Upon retirement, active members may remain members in good standing or withdraw to honorary membership.

## INTERNATIONAL ASSOCIATION OF CHIEF'S OF POLICE

In the early years of law enforcement, nearly everywhere, industrialization, immigration, and urbanization were creating problems of great complexity. Among them was a strong increase in crime. Police were almost helpless against increasing crime. Professional criminals were better organized than the agencies which fought them.

Law enforcement executives understood better than anyone else how unsatisfactory all this was. In 1893 these executives joined together to create a professional association. The first police chief's organization had fifty-one members and no full-time staff.

Today the International Association of Chiefs of Police (IACP) has grown to 8,000 members and includes police executives from city, county, state, and national law enforcement agencies in the United States, Canada, and sixty other nations. Its active members are command level police officers in public law agencies, and associate membership is open to anyone qualified by training or experience, including police personnel below command level, academic professionals, public officials, prosecuting attorneys, and others.

The IACP is incorporated as a tax-exempt nonprofit organization. Through grants from and contracts with agencies at every level of government, through membership fees, publications sales, foundation grants, and contributions, it provides research and consulting services unique in law enforcement. It is the only organization concerned exclusively with professionalization of the police. Some aims and objectives of IACP are (1) to advance the science and art of police services, (2) to develop and disseminate improved administrative, technical, and operational practices and promote their use in police work, (3) to foster police cooperation and the exchange of information and experience among police administrations throughout the world, (4) to bring about recruitment and training in the police profession of qualified persons, and (5) to encourage adherence of all police officers to high professional standards of performance and conduct.

IACP has initiated many projects, one being *crime check,* which is a public education program for police departments. This program urges citizens to report to police crimes being committed, as well as informing them about basic steps individuals can take to increase protection for themselves and their property. Other projects IACP has started and backed are police vehicle standards which would develop different automobiles for specific police activities, emergency telephone numbers, legal assistance, crime prevention, and police community relations programs.

## INTERNATIONAL ASSOCIATION FOR IDENTIFICATION

The International Association for Identification (IAI) was founded in Oakland, California, in 1915, by a group of identification specialists. At this time its membership consisted of 1,500 members; recently it has grown to 1,700 members, with representation in each of the 50 states and in 64 foreign countries.

The purpose of this organization is to improve methods of fingerprinting and other scientific identification techniques used in criminal and civil investigation, and to work for mandatory fingerprinting of all persons.

At the time that IAI was founded, identification and other police sciences as we now know them are either in their infancy or completely unknown. The need to explore this new world was greater in the twenties than ever, with the increasing amount of crime. These identification specialists proposed to meet annually to advance the growth and promotion of such knowledge. IAI's membership now includes the leading identification men throughout the world.

Besides encouraging research work in scientific crime detection, other aims and objectives of IAI are (1) to associate persons who are engaged in the profession of identification, investigation, and scientific examination of physical evidence in an organized body so that the profession and its branches may be standardized and effectively practiced, (2) to encourage the enlargement and improvement of the science of fingerprinting and other branches of crime detection, (3) to keep its members informed of the latest techniques and discoveries in crime detection, (4) to employ the collective wisdom of the profession, and (5) to educate legislative bodies concerning the need for general laws making it mandatory for every person to be fingerprinted.

IAI publishes a monthly sixteen-page magazine *Identification News* which is distributed to its members. This magazine brings the latest news of interest to its members and makes them acquainted with the newest equipment, techniques, and methods in the field.

Persons eligible for membership in IAI consist of heads of bureaus of identification or investigation, heads of police departments, chief of detectives and sheriffs, provided that the persons are bona fide employees of and receive salaries from national, state, county, or municipal governments, or some subdivision thereof.

## INTERNATIONAL CONFERENCE OF POLICE ASSOCIATIONS

This organization was the National Conference of Police Associations, until July 12, 1965, when its name was changed to include International.

The origin of the association began in March of 1953 when the Detroit Police Officers Association took it upon themselves to try and form a national organization of police officers. On April 7,

1954, after other interested departments and associations responded to Detroit's call, the National Conference of Police Associations was incorporated and came into being.

From this modest beginning the ICPA has grown to be one of the largest organizations of its kind in the world. The ICPA represents over 140,000 police officers throughout the U.S., Canada, and the Panama Canal Zone.

The main purpose of the association is to professionalize law enforcement and act as a common front, utilizing planned representation in Washington, D.C. for the benefit of all law enforcement, while still respecting the autonomy of the individual police organizations.

The object and purpose of the association shall be to collect, study, standardize, summarize, and to disseminate factual data for the professionalization of the police service, and to stimulate mutual cooperation between law enforcement agencies.

Among the benefits offered members are a monthly newsletter, permanent legislative advocate before the Congress of the United States to protect the rights of police officers, latest data in regard to retirement systems, and exchange of information between member organizations.

Membership is not open to individuals, but rather to individual bona fide police associations only. Any organizations composed of full-time, sworn, law enforcement officers who are members of any organized local, county, or state retirement system are eligible.

Basically, the ICPA is a conference of police associations working freely and spontaneously together for the best interests of the members, with a constant view toward the advancement, promotion, and upgrading of the police service.

## INTERNATIONAL NARCOTIC ENFORCEMENT OFFICERS ASSOCIATION (I.N.E.O.A.)

The I.N.E.O.A. was founded in 1960 by John J. Bellizzi in Albany, New York. The organization is composed of officials from all levels of government, representing over 13,000 narcotic enforcement officers, medical and public health officials, educators and representatives of drug industries from over 120 countries throughout the world, with membership in every state throughout the United States, every province of Canada, and every country in South America. Former U.S. Narcotic Commissioner Harry J. Anslinger, now serving as U.S. Narcotic Representative to the United Nations is president of the association. The association was organized to coordinate law enforcement methods on a national and international scale and to aid authoritatives in establishing educational programs for law enforcement officers, students, and the general public.

The organization brings together law enforcement officers and officials with members of the medical profession, drug manufacturers, and educators who, through united efforts, seek to combat the evils of drug abuse and addiction, especially among teenagers. Cooperation with all related law enforcement agencies, governmental bodies, and the medical profession, to include drug manufacturers and pharmaceutical firms, has led to the development of educational films, training seminars, and the creation and passage of vital legislation on a national and international scale.

1. Members receive a monthly newletter which contains the latest Supreme Court decisions on narcotic violation cases and results on current views on search and seizure methods. Training aids to narcotic investigations are reviewed and special discounts to members of I.N.E.O.A. are made available.

2. The latest methods of smuggling are disclosed and outstanding cases are summarized to publicize law enforcement officers' dedication to duty.

3. The latest educational and research material on a certain drug or narcotic is published to keep members ever informed and current.

4. Legislation that is pending or recently passed that affects members is summarized.

5. All members receive an Annual Conference Report which contains the latest narcotics information on a worldwide basis by the top men throughout the world.

6. An annual conference is held for all members in October for training seminars and general fellowship.

7. Each member is furnished an I.D. card, lapel pin, and a Directory of Membership listing all members by title and agency and their address, with the invitation to contact them in the event help is needed anywhere in the free world.

## INTERNATIONAL JUVENILE OFFICERS ASSOCIATION

This organization was activated in March, 1957. The purposes are to encourage participation in all matters that have to do with youths and their problems, as they pertain to the field of law enforcement; to assist in the furthering of the interest of its members and bring about understanding and cooperation with the various youth service agencies; to encourage the application of the highest ethical standards of the profession and to endeavor, by the exchange of methods and ideas, to increase efficiency within the local organization of juvenile officers.

Active membership is limited to persons who are law enforcement officers interested in the field of handling offenses committed by or against youth. Associate membership is open to persons in allied fields and have the same interest in juveniles as active members.

Proven techniques of organization are known by members of the International Juvenile Officers Association which they will share with other police agencies upon request. They will also assist in instituting these practices. The members are trained and experienced to aid states and communities to organize citizen groups who are interested in their state and community problems, relating to youth and also in reorganizing law enforcement agencies' youth divisions if it is desired locally.

Members of the association have aided in establishing a standard recording system for juvenile offenders in many states. This type of recording aids in the prevention of delinquency through better records. The juvenile records have been extremely inconsistent and lacking in reporting juvenile delinquency, crime, and court cases. Intra-access to juvenile files has been restricted to protect the offender. The association has encouraged the establishment of a central record file for police agencies in large and small jurisdictions, so that police can keep pace with today's mobile youth.

The association tries to consistently keep law enforcement personnel aware of the need for up-to-date training, to provide opportunities for law enforcement personnel to attend training institutes. This can be done by providing institutes throughout the nation on a regional basis. The police, more than any other agency, are aware of the problems youth are facing in today's complex society. The only way we can efficiently cope with the problem is to be prepared and to train not only the special juvenile officer, but also get basic information to all police officers and agencies as well. This can be done by making more institutes available through scholarships, grants, and state and local cooperation.

Members of the association will continue to maintain an active interest and support in local, state, and federal legislation which affects the young people and as it affects law enforcement. In the same manner, opposition to certain legislative programs when it is evident that the desired result of such legislative programs would not be constructive for our youth or for the efficiency of law enforcement or cooperating agencies.

The association maintains an effective public relations program with all agencies having similar goals and objectives and the news media. They publish and distribute educational material designed to inform law enforcement and other agencies on all matters of concern. The association will encourage greater respect for law enforcement and authority through extensive public information programs and by our own ethics, and to carry out programs, projects, and activities approved by the Board of Governors. An example of such an effort for greater respect for law enforcement was a letter sent from the association to the president of Chrysler Motors criticizing the commercial with the Dodge Charger and the caricature of the police officer. The position of the association was that the commercial was offensive and that they would boycott all Chrysler products until the commercial was removed.

Members of the association will aid in and conduct surveys and research for the purpose of finding ways and means by which we can unite our efforts with other enforcement agencies, youth, and other agencies whereby states and communities can be assisted to make better use of their facilities so that more youth can take advantage of all opportunities.

It appears that this association is well organized and has desirable goals. They have been conducting annual training conferences in various parts of the country since their activation. Some of their objectives that apply to youth in their organization apply to the police profession as a whole.

## THE MILITARY POLICE ASSOCIATION

The MPA was formed at the U.S. Army Military Police School in 1951 to fill the need for an association which serves law enforcement personnel of the armed forces. Today the association has a membership of over 14,000 in the United States and over 40 different countries.

The goals of the organization are to advance the science of police administration and crime prevention and to preserve and foster the spirit of fellowship among former, present, and future law enforcement personnel of the armed forces and other persons interested in the police profession.

The national organization headquarters is located at the U. S. Army Military Police School, Ft. Gordon, Georgia, with local chapters located everywhere in the world that a U.S. Army Military Police unit is stationed.

The MPA sponsors many seminars each year which bring together both military and civilian law enforcement officers from all over the world.

Social functions are held for the general membership as well as recreational events for underprivileged children in the area of Augusta, Georgia. The MPA publishes a monthly magazine, *The Military Police Journal,* which is both informative and educational in nature.

The membership is open to all persons who have been or may be engaged in law enforcement and to any other persons interested in the objectives of the association.

## LIST OF SOURCES AND ADDRESSES

The following is a list of organizations and their current

addresses which was used as a source of material for this chapter.

Association of Former OSI, S/A, Inc.
P.O. Box 2337
Anaheim, California, 92804

Fraternal Order of Police
1012 Prospect Ave.
Cleveland, Ohio, 44115

International Association of Chiefs of Police
1319 18th St. N.W.
Washington, D.C., 20036

International Association for Identification
P.O. Box 139
Utica, New York, 13503

International Conference of Police Associations
1241 Penn Ave. S.E.
Washington, D.C., 20003

International Narcotic Enforcement Officer Association
178 Washington Ave.
Albany, New York, 12210

International Juvenile Officers Association
P.O. Box 426
West Bend, Wisconsin, 53095

Military Police Association
P.O. Box 3385
Augusta, Georgia, 30904

National Police Officers' Association
1890 S. Tamiami Trail
Venice, Florida, 33595

National Police Reserve Officers' Association
Headquarters Bldg. Suite 615
Washington, D.C., 20036

# BIBLIOGRAPHY

## BOOKS

Almond, Gabriel Abraham, The Appeals of Communism. Princeton, Princeton, N.J., 1954.

Bartlett, John Henry, The Bonas March And The New Deal. M.A. Donohue, Chicago, 1957.

Bernstein, Irving, et al., Emergency Disputes And National Policy. Harper & Bros., New York, 1955.

Black, Algermann, The Police And Politics. McGraw-Hill, New York, 1968.

Bouscaren, Anthony T., A Guide To Anti-Communist Action. Henry Regnery, Chicago, 1958.

Brandstatter, A.F., and Radelet, Louis A., Police Community Relations: A Source Book, Glencoe Press, Glencoe, Ill., 1968.

Bristow, Allen, Effective Police Manpower Utilization, Thomas, Springfield, 1969.

Brown, Thorvald, The Enigma of Drug Addiction. Thomas, Springfield, 1961.

Burns & Peltason, Government By The People. Prentice-Hall, Englewood Cliffs, N.J., 1960.

Chevigny, Paul, Police Power. Pantheon Books, New York, 1969.

Clark, Donald E., and Chapman, Samuel, G., A Forward Step. Thomas, Springfield, 1966.

Clark, F.G., How To Be Popular Though Conservative. Van Nostrand, Princeton, N.J., 1948.

Cohn-Bendit, Daniel, Obsolete Communism. McGraw-Hill, New York, 1968.

Cook, Fred J., The Secret Rulers. Duell, Sloan & Pearce, Des Moines, 1966.

Daniels, R.V., The Nature Of Communism. Random House, New York, 1962.

Djilas, Milovan, The New Class — An Analysis Of The Communist System. Praeger, New York, 1966.

Earle, Howard H., Police-Community Relations. Thomas, Springfield, 1967.

Fisher, Harold H., The Communist Revolution — An Outline Of Strategy And Tactics. Stanford, Stanford, 1955.

Garner, Erle Stanley, Cops On Campus And Crime In The Streets. William Morrow and Co., New York, 1970.

Gourley, Douglas G., Public Relations And The Police. Thomas, Springfield, 1953.

Hollingsworth, Dan, Rocks In The Roadway. Stromberg Allen & Co., Chicago, 1954.

Hoover, J. Edgar, A Study Of Communism. Holt, Rinehart and Winston, New York, 1962.

Hoover, J. Edgar, Espionage-Contemporary Communism. Wadsworth, Belmont, Calif., 1963.

Hoover, J. Edgar, Masters Of Deceit. Henry Holt & Co., New York, 1958.

Howe, Irving, and Coses, Lewis, The American Communist Party — A Critical History. Beacon Press, Boston, 1958.

International City Manager's Association, Municipal Police Administration. Cushing-Malloy, Ann Arbor, 1969.

Jacker, Corinne, The Black Flag Of Anarchy. Scribner, New York, 1968.

Jacobs, D.N., The New Communists. Harper & Row, New York, 1969.

Kooken, Don L., Ethics In Police Service. Thomas, Springfield, 1957.

Lane, Roger, Policing The City. Harvard, Cambridge, 1967.

Mass, Peter, The Valachi Papers. Bantam Books, New York, 1969.

Merriam and Goetz, Going Into Politics. Harper, New York, 1957.

Messick, Hank, The Silent Syndicate. MacMillan, New York, 1967.

Moley, Raymond, Politics And Criminal Prosecution. Minton, Balch and Co., New York, 1929.

Mills, G.W., The Marxists. Dell, New York, 1962.

Momboisse, Raymond M., Community Relations And Riot Prevention. Thomas, Springfield, 1967.

Niederhoffer, Arthur, Behind The Shield: The Police In Urban Society. Doubleday, Garden City, N.Y., 1969.

Pantaleone, Michele, The Mafia And Politics. Coward-McCann, New York, 1966.

Pound, Roscoe, Criminal Justice In America. Holt & Co., New York, 1930.

Reid, Ed., The Grim Reapers. Henry Regency Co., Chicago, 1969.

Reith, Charles, The Blind Eye Of History. Faber & Faber, London, 1952.

Salerno, Ralph, and Tomkins, John, The Crime Confederation. Doubleday, New York, 1969.

Schultz, Donald O. and Norton, Loran A., Police Operational Intelligence. Thomas, Springfield, 1968.

Skousen, W.G., The Naked Communist. Ensign, Salt Lake City, 1961.

Smith, Bruce, Police Systems In U.S. Harper, New York, 1949.

Turner, William, The Police Establishment. Putnam, New York, 1968.

United States Chamber of Commerce, Deskbook On Organized Crime. Washington, D.C., 1969.

Van Allen, Edward J., Our Handcuffed Police. Reportorial Press, Mineola, N.Y., 1968.

Volz, Joseph and Bridge, Peter J., The Mafia Talks. Fawcett, Greenwich, Conn., 1969.

Warren, F.A., Liberals and Communism. Indiana Univ., Bloomington, 1966.

Wege, Nathaniel, The Battle Against Disloyalties. Thomas Y. Crowell, New York, 1951.

Weston, Paul, The Police Traffic Control Function. Thomas, Springfield, 1969.

## MAGAZINE ARTICLES

A death in the family. Life, Feb. 28, 1969.

Allen, Gary, Red teachers. American Opinion, Feb., 1969.

Another target of new left – the armed forces. U.S. News & World Report, May 26, 1969.

An answer from a student activist. US New & World Report, June 16, 1969.

Atwater, James, Detroit vs the Mafia. Saturday Evening Post, May 30, 1964.

Berube, Maurice R., Black power and the clearing process. Commonwealth, April, 1969.

Bettelheim, Bruno, Obsolete youth. Encounter, Sept., 1969.

Big Tab. Newsweek, Oct. 3, 1966.

Big Spender, Newsweek, Oct. 14, 1963.

Bloy, Myron R., Jr., Culture and counter culture. Commonwealth, Jan., 1969.

Brann, James, National rally for student power. Nation, Dec. 18, 1967.

Brazen empire of crime: from a governor and a D.A., an offer of resignation. Life, Sept. 29, 1967.

Burn the mother down. The Saturday Evening Post, Nov. 16, 1968.

Campus violence. US News & World Report, Sept. 1, 1969.

Catlin, Robert E., Should public employees have the right to strike? Public Personnel Review, Jan., 1968.

Copp, William C., Let no one be fooled! Law And Order, Jan., 1959.

Cosa Nostra, the poison in our society. Reader's Digest, Dec., 1969.

Crime: kiss of death. Newsweek, Oct. 7, 1963.

Crime our thing. Newsweek, Aug. 19, 1963.

Draper, Theodore, The ghost of social-fascism. Commentary, Feb., 1969.

Ellinger, Rory V., Decline and fall of a student movement. Commonwealth, Jan., 1969.

End to big riots. US News & World Report, June 2, 1969.

Green, Mark, Reparations for Blacks. Commonwealth, June, 1969.

Gumaer, David Emerson, The A.C.L.U. American Opinion, Sept., 1969.

Gumaer, David Emerson, Sabotage. American Opinion,

Hare, Nathan, Black. Rampart, July, 1969.

Harris, Sheldon, San Fernanado's Black revolt. Commonwealth, Jan., 1969.

Hatch, John, Black studies: the real issue. Nation, June 16, 1969.

Hearings. Newsweek, Oct. 14, 1963.

Hoover, J. Edgar, Message from the Director. FBI Law Enforcement Bulletin, Sept., 1968.

How Mafia killers got their man. Saturday Evening Post, Oct. 31, 1964.

How the Mob controls Chicago. Saturday Evening Post, Nov. 9, 1963.

Investigations: Jersey bounce. Newsweek, Dec. 22, 1969.

Italy: a mother's pain. Newsweek, May 2, 1960.

Italy: guilty friars. Newsweek, July 15, 1963.

Italy: justice for Francia. Newsweek, Jan. 2, 1967.

Italy: Let them kill me. Newsweek, May 6, 1963.

Italy: the Sicilian canary. Newsweek, Oct. 14, 1963.

Jacobs, James, SDS – between reform and revolution. Nation, June 10, 1968.

Kassalow, Everett M. Trade unionism goes public. The Public Interest, Winter, 1969.

Kelman, Steven, Beyond new leftism. Commentary, Feb., 1969.

Kheel, Theodore W., Can we stand strikes by teachers, police, garbage men, etc? Readers Digest, Aug., 1969.

Kreutzer, Walter E., The elusive professionalization that police officers seek. The Police Chief, Aug., 1969.

Lacqueur, Walter, Reflections on youth movements. Commentary, June, 1969.

Lawder, Lee E., From the editor. Law And Order, Feb., 1959.

Legislative bulletin. Valor, June, 1967.

Lutz, Carl F., Overcoming obstacles to professionalism. The Police Chief, Sept., 1968.

Mafia rubs out a rebellion. Life, Aug. 30, 1963.

Mafia: the inside story. Saturday Evening Post, Aug. 10, 1963.

Martin, P.W., The draft card burners. Nation, July 22, 1968.

Mass, Peter, The story behind the crime hearings. Saturday Evening Post, Nov. 23, 1963.

McClellan, John L., Weak link in our war on the Mafia. Readers Digest, March, 1970.

McWilliam, Cary, Protest, power and the future of politics. Nation, Jan. 15, 1968.

More, Harry W., The era of police collective bargaining. Law And Order, June, 1969.

Murdy, Ralph G., Civilian review boards in review. FBI Law Enforcement Bulletin, July, 1966.

Neoling, Sgt. Floyd M., The police pay problem: a solution. Law And Order, Oct., 1969.

O'Brien, William P., Unionization of police is main topic at ICPA annual conference. The Law Officer, Fall, 1969.

Oppenheimer, Martin, Strategies for the ghetto wars. Nation, Mar. 24, 1969.

Pomerleau, Donald D., The eleventh hour. The Police Chief, Dec., 1969.

Russian strategy against the United States. US News & World Report, June 16, 1969.

Schultz, Donald O., Police review boards. Valor, Dec., 1969.

Schultz, Donald O., Police Unions. Valor, April, 1970.

Singleton, Donald, How organized crime takes over business. The American Legion Magazine, April, 1970.

Skousen, W. C., What about police labor unions? Law And Order, Oct., 1966.

Smith, Sandy, The crime cartel. Life, Sept. 1, 1967.

Snow, C.P., Liberal communism. Nation, Dec. 9, 1968.

The call of the Black Panther. The New York Times, Aug. 6, 1969.

The conglomerate of crime. Time, Aug. 22, 1969.

The crime syndicate. Newsweek, April 14, 1969.

The Four Friars. Newsweek, March 26, 1962.

The Panther's bite. Time, Sept. 20, 1968.

Warning of revolutionary change. US News & World Report, May 26, 1969.

Where the Attorney General draws the line on SDS and violence. US News & World Report, June 2, 1969.

Widmer, Kingslen, Why dissent turns violent. Nation, April, 7, 1969.

Williams, Gerald O., Historical origins and development of political police. Police, March, 1969.

Winckoski, Bernard G., The name of the game is collective bargaining. The Police Chief, Dec., 1969.

Wyrick, Ed, Editors comment. Wisconsin Police Chief, Jan., 1970.


## NEWSPAPERS

City's police face peril of snipers daily. Chicago Tribune, Mar. 22, 1970.

Inside Huey Newton. The Black Panther News Service, Aug. 6, 1969.

Law a shield for organized crime. Omaha World Herald, Jan. 24, 1970.

Mafia thrives on fear, expands on legal loopholes. Progress Bulletin, (Pomona, Calif.) March 27, 1969.

Mafia unlimited. Omaha World Herald, Jan. 25, 1970.


## BROCHURES

International Association For Identification, Miami, Florida.

International Association Of Chief's Of Police, Washington, D.C.

International Conference Of Police Associations, Washington, D.C.

The Fraternal Order Of Police, Cleveland, Ohio.

The National Police Officer's Association, Venice, Florida.


## DEPARTMENTAL DIRECTIVES AND GENERAL ORDERS

Baltimore Police Department, Code of Rules, Baltimore, Maryland.

Charlotte Police Department, General Order #11, The Use of Force by Police Officer, Charlotte, North Carolina.

Charlotte Police Department, Training Bulletin #7, _____ _____, Charlotte, North Carolina.

Charlotte Police Department, Information Bulletin #31, The Chemical Mace, Charlotte, North Carolina, October 11, 1967.

Department of the Army, Pamphlet #360-81, To Insure Domestic Tranquility, Washington, 1968.

Department of the Army, Field Manual #19-15, Civil Disturbances and Disasters, Washington, 1968.

Kansas City Police Department, General Order #68-32, K-9 Squad, Kansas City, Missouri, 1968.

Kansas City Police Department, Memorandum #67-10, Use of Mace, Kansas City, Missouri.

Kansas City Police Department, Memorandum 67-37, Discharge of Firearms, Kansas City, Missouri, 1967.

Kansas City Police Department, Procedural Instructions #69-4, Control of Civil Disorder, Kansas City, Missouri, 1969.

Kansas City Police Department, Code of Rules.

United States Army Military Police School, pamphlet, A Platoon Leader's Guide for Civil Disturbance Operations, Fort Gordon, 1968.

## OTHER SOURCES

Juris, Harvey A., and Hutchison, Kay B., The Legal Status Of Municipal Police Employee Organizations. Working Paper No. 2, University of Wisconsin, July, 1969.

National Commission On Violence, The Politics Of Protest. U.S. Government Printing Office, 1969.

Presidents Commission On Law Enforcement, 1967, Task Force Report. Government Printing Office, 1967.

Newsletter, International Narcotic Enforcement Officer's Association Albany, New York.

Rarick, Hon. John R., Sensitivity training. Congressional Record, House of Representatives, March 11, 1969.

Smoot, Dan, Vol 16   #19-24, The Smooth Report.

Staff Report to the President, Rights In Concord. U.S. Government, Jan. 18, 1969.

The FBI Annual Report, 1969.

# INDEX

175